"I have come to the conclusion that success is predictable and so is failure. This is because life was designed to function by laws. Laws make the results predictable. Therefore, those who learn these laws and apply them will experience success in any culture. Talayah, in *Light Bulb Moments,* has distilled many of these laws and put them in reach for everyone to access. Enjoy every page and watch your life move to the top."

—Dr. Myles Munroe, founding chairman of the International Third World Leaders Association, Nassau, Bahamas

"Talayah and I share more than the same last name. We have a passion for helping real people discover the miraculous, magic moments in everyday life. Through a series of vignettes, Talayah opens the door so we can all experience the possibilities."

—Jim Stovall, author of *The Ultimate Gift*

"Wow, I simply love this book. Seldom does a book say it better or more powerfully than *Light Bulb Moments.* This book is a must-read for all those who want to navigate the slippery slopes of living a successful life and self-sufficiency. My heartfelt thanks go out to Talayah Stovall for giving us this timely and important gem."

—George C. Fraser, author of *Success Runs in Our Race* and *CLICK*

LIGHT BULB
MOMENTS

Also by Talayah G. Stovall

Books

CROSSING THE THRESHOLD: Opening Your Door to Successful Relationships

150 IMPORTANT QUESTIONS YOU SHOULD ASK BEFORE YOU SAY "I DO"

CDs

P.U.M.P. IT UP!

7 SECRETS TO IGNITE YOUR DREAMS

LIGHT BULB MOMENTS

75 Lessons for Everyday Living

TALAYAH G. STOVALL

FOREWORD BY LES BROWN,
AUTHOR OF *LIVE YOUR DREAMS*

HAY HOUSE, INC.
Carlsbad, California • New York City
London • Sydney • Johannesburg
Vancouver • Hong Kong • New Delhi

Published and distributed in the United States by: Hay House, Inc.:
www.hayhouse.com® • *Published and distributed in Australia by:*
Hay House Australia Pty. Ltd.: www.hayhouse.com.au • *Published
and distributed in the United Kingdom by:* Hay House UK, Ltd.: www
.hayhouse.co.uk • *Published and distributed in the Republic of South
Africa by:* Hay House SA (Pty), Ltd.: www.hayhouse.co.za • *Distributed
in Canada by:* Raincoast Books: www.raincoast.com • *Published in
India by:* Hay House Publishers India: www.hayhouse.co.in

Cover design: Karla Baker • *Interior design:* Nick C. Welch

Cataloging-in-Publication Data is on file at the Library of Congress.

Tradepaper ISBN: 978-1-4019-4392-9

17 16 15 14   4 3 2 1
1st edition, June 2014

Printed in the United States of America

To God, who is my constant Source of inspiration.

*To the many family members and dear friends who
have supported me along life's journey. Thanks for
your love and support and for being with me as
I lived and learned from all of the lessons in this book.*

*To my new friends. Thank you for supporting this book.
I hope to meet you very soon.*

CONTENTS

FOREWORD

Les Brown, motivational speaker and author of *Live Your Dreams*

It's been said that there's no shortage of opportunity; there's a shortage of ideas. This book, *Light Bulb Moments,* is about becoming more innovative in our thinking and open to the possibility of creating more and having more. It's about developing a mind-set of optimism, of unlimited possibilities of how we can begin to create a future that we can feel proud of. And it starts by having a vision of yourself and thinking from a place of power and creativity to create your own reality.

My favorite book says, "Be ye not conformed to this world, but be ye transformed by the renewing of your mind." *Light Bulb Moments* will challenge you. It will allow you to begin to think beyond your circumstances and mental conditioning and inspire you to pursue your greatness.

It has also been said that opportunity knocks on every door. Well, *Light Bulb Moments* challenges us and says that opportunity does not knock on every door. It stands by silently, waiting for us to recognize it.

My name is Les Brown, and I'm the author of *Live Your Dreams. Light Bulb Moments* will change your life as it has changed mine. That's my story, and I'm sticking to it.

INTRODUCTION

"Earth and sky, woods and fields, lakes and rivers, the mountain and the sea, are excellent schoolmasters, and teach some of us more than we can ever learn from books."

JOHN LUBBOCK (ENGLISH BIOLOGIST AND POLITICIAN, 1834–1913)

Have you ever had one of those experiences when the light bulb just went off? You thought to yourself, *Now I get it! That was the lesson I was supposed to learn in all of this!* I tend to get many such revelations when I'm experiencing nature. There's something about water, trees, and mountains that makes me feel more in touch with the Creator and more able to make sense out of the complexities of life.

Regardless of our vocation, gender, or nationality, we have more in common than we have differences. We all have mothers, uncles, teachers, and friends who have influenced our lives. We all have experienced joy and sorrow, health and sickness, love and loss. We all have overcome obstacles and endured pain. There have been times when we've wanted to give up—on a job, a business, a relationship, a child, or even our health. The important thing, especially when coming out of a challenging period (a *valley experience*, as they're sometimes called), is not to lose the lesson.

Light Bulb Moments is a series of vignettes that shares life lessons I learned through everyday occurrences. They focus on topics such as purpose, passion, preparation, persistence, patience, goal focus, trials, forgiveness, friendship, and more. There are many more stories that I wish I'd written while they were fresh on my mind. But, I also know there are many more lessons to come.

Writing was and is still my first love. When I began my "EmPOWERed to . . ." newsletter several years ago, I found it gratifying and humbling when readers would write to tell me how my stories spoke to current situations in their own lives. It made me feel as if my words could make a difference.

I hope that some of my life lessons will resonate with you, as well. Enjoy!

Talayah

PREPARE, PERSEVERE, AND IT WILL PASS

"I do not think there is any other quality so essential to success of any kind as the quality of perseverance. It overcomes almost everything, even nature."

JOHN D. ROCKEFELLER

Well, it was my bright idea, so I really can't complain. And it seemed like such a good idea at the time . . .

On a visit to Saint Martin, I took an excursion to a nearby island called Saba. Expecting a lush, tropical paradise, I was surprised to find that there were no beaches, and what they tried to pass off as shopping left much to be desired. It happens that the only real activities on Saba are scuba diving and climbing an extinct volcano. I've been scuba diving before, and it was a wonderful experience; however, since I do not know how to swim (at all!), I decided

1

not to push my luck by trying it again. Besides, the nature lover in me was excited about conquering the mountain. It is said that from the top, one can see seven surrounding islands. It sounded like the experience of a lifetime to me. Anyway, the mountain didn't look very daunting.

As I got out of the van, I decided to lighten my load as much as possible. I began to take out the nonessential items. Figuring that the heavy bottle of water I had would only slow me down, I took one last swig and left it inside the van. Our group of about 16 began to climb the 1,000-plus stairs and winding paths that led to the top of the mountain. Those days when I'd skipped the gym were beginning to show, and it wasn't long before I yearned for the water I'd left behind. Definitely, this was a lesson about the importance of preparation for a journey.

As we made our way up the mountain, the group began to split up. People started drifting from the friends they'd come with and making new friends along the path. We began bonding—joking with and encouraging each other. As I climbed higher and higher, my own group became smaller and smaller. Some people went on ahead; others dropped out. Soon I found myself traveling with a man whose pace matched mine. We'd forge ahead and then stop to rest, taking pictures and chatting, just to give ourselves an excuse to linger longer.

Soon my new friend decided to head back down, and I had to decide whether to continue on alone or go back, as well. I decided that since I'd come all that way to climb the mountain, I would indeed climb it. I couldn't stand the thought that I might be close to the top and give up before I got there. So I pressed on, hot, thirsty, and tired, rather than admit defeat.

As I walked on alone, I began to think of the journey we make through life. We start out with friends and loved ones beside us, but at some point our pace no longer matches theirs and we have to go it alone. Sometimes our friends will leave us, and sometimes we must leave them. But if we all keep pressing onward and upward, we'll make it to the top. Although we feel alone, we know that God is with us, and that gives us the strength to persevere. With that in mind, I had more determination to make it to the top.

I watched, expectantly, hoping to meet someone coming down the mountain so I could ask how much longer I had to travel. At one point, I spotted what I thought was the top of the mountain and was very encouraged, only to realize that what I was looking at was not the top. I couldn't even see the top yet.

Finally, I met a couple coming back down the path. I asked them how much farther I had to climb. They grinned and the man said, "About ten minutes. You can make it. It's beautiful up there. We saw all seven islands!"

I thought, *I can do it!* I walked on a little farther and could finally make out the top of the mountain. I was so excited, until I rounded the bend and noticed that the path led down into a small valley. I stood and looked down the path, feeling very discouraged. For a brief moment, I even considered turning back. I knew that if I went down into the valley, I'd have to climb back up again just to get to my current elevation. Ever heard of a setback? The good thing about setbacks is that they're temporary. The bad thing is that you've still got to go through them. The playwright Edward Albee once wrote, "Sometimes it's necessary to go a long distance out of the way in order to come back a short distance correctly." Just when you think you've almost achieved your goal—you've almost reached the success you seek, you've almost got enough money to cover the bills, you've almost got that new job or contract—you find yourself in another valley and you have to climb back out all over again. But you can never just quit because you never know how close you might be.

With that in mind, I marched with determination down into the valley and climbed back up the other side. I ran into a few more people on their way back down. I asked them, "How much farther do I have to go?" They said, "Not far. About five minutes. You can do it; you're almost there!" I believed that I could and pressed on. A friend of mine (who was obviously in better shape than me) was in the group and agreed to go back up with me. I was grateful for the company and the support, and I enjoyed hearing again about the beautiful view that awaited me. God brings the right people into your life at just the right time to encourage you and help you on your journey.

I soon learned that in order to reach the very top, you have to climb the last portion of the mountain by pulling up on a rope. That part was actually quite easy and fun (of course, going back down the rope was another matter entirely). I quickly scrambled up the rope.

I couldn't wait to see the spectacular view I'd heard so much about. Unfortunately, though, by the time I got to the top of the mountain, clouds had rolled in and visibility was almost zero. I couldn't see anything more than a few feet in front of my face. I was also expecting there to be a spacious expanse of land at the top. Wrong again. The mountaintop was about as big as my closet, and it looked out at nothing but clouds. Ever been disappointed when you finally got "there" and "there" wasn't what you thought it was going to be?

I was hot, I was tired, I was thirsty, and I still had to go back down the mountain. At first I was disappointed that reaching the top was not at all what I'd expected. Then I considered the life lessons I'd learned:

- **Always prepare for the journey.** Get in shape, and don't leave your water bottle behind.

- **Don't quit.** Persevere, even when you have to climb alone.

- **March on through the valleys.** Sometimes you have to pass through a valley to get to the mountaintop.

Days later, when I could walk normally again, I discovered how much more toned my legs had become as a result of the climb. I was much stronger and in better shape than I'd been before I had climbed the mountain. It was then that I realized yet another lesson:

- Sometimes the reward is not in reaching the mountaintops of life but in the lessons you learn during your journey and the strength you gain from the climb.

Whether we choose our mountains or whether the mountains in our lives appear in front of us, it is up to us to decide how we handle the obstacles that block our paths to success. Don't be afraid to tackle the mountains!

LET THE SEASONINGS COME TOGETHER

"Patience, persistence, and perspiration make an unbeatable combination for success."

NAPOLEON HILL

At breakfast one day, my friend Angie was telling me about the really good soup she'd made the week before (yes, we were eating while talking about eating). She said it was the first time that it had taken her four days to make a pot of soup. She started on Tuesday, cutting up the peppers. On Wednesday, she added some chicken broth to the peppers and decided to let it sit until the next day so that the flavors would all meld together. She added vegetables and chicken and tasted it again on Thursday, but she felt it still wasn't quite ready, much to her family's chagrin (they'd already been waiting two days for the soup). She decided to wait another day. She tasted it on Friday and it was pretty good, but it was still missing something. She determined that rice was what it needed. After tasting it with the rice, she declared that it was delicious and served it to her family. They agreed it was the best soup she'd ever made. (Believe me, I put my bid in for a bowl and I agreed with their assessment.)

As Angie was telling the story of the soup, a light bulb went off for me. I thought, *Isn't that a great example of the kind of patience, diligence, and care that we should use in all areas of our lives?* So often we throw things together, relationships, careers, or businesses, and expect instant results. We want everything to come together in a perfectly delicious manner without us ever having to wait for all the seasonings to blend. We're used to pressing that button on the microwave and getting immediate gratification. But if we would just put in the necessary work and allow the right amount of time for things to meld together, we would get much better results.

The lesson I received from Angie's soup story is that if we really want what is best for us in life, we have to be willing to:

- **Take things a step at a time.** Anything that is really worth having is worth waiting for. Instead of expecting instant satisfaction, go through the necessary steps to put things together the right way.

- **"Taste" as you go to see how things are coming along.** Whether we're working on building our finances or building a relationship, whether we're completing a project at work or one at home, we have to constantly check our progress to make sure we're still on track. Put some measures in place so that you'll know you're making progress in the right direction.

- **Don't declare that it is done until it is seasoned exactly how you want it to be.** Stop settling for okay and hold out for excellent.

- **Share it when it's done.** It's wonderful to see a plan through to fruition and to appreciate the work you've done. But it's always more enjoyable when you have someone to share it with.

THE RAINBOW ONLY COMES AFTER THE STORM

*"May God give you . . . For every storm a rainbow,
for every tear a smile, for every care a
promise and a blessing in each trial."*

IRISH BLESSING

Traveling in Honolulu, I was amazed not only by the number of rainbows that were visible, but by the fullness of the rainbows. I'd seen rainbows in Chicago, but these were different. These were complete horseshoe-shaped arcs, and the colors were so intense that I was tempted to look for the pot of gold at the other end (of course, I had no idea which end that might be). On one day in particular, it seemed as if we were about to drive right through the middle of a rainbow that straddled the freeway. I thought about my high school physics class. "The colors of the rainbow, Roy G. Biv," Mr. Koloff would chant with his hands on his hips, eyes blinking. "Red, orange, yellow, green, blue, indigo, violet." (Thanks to that little tip, I never forgot the sequence.) Sure enough, all seven colors were present and in their proper order in the clear afternoon sky. Mr. Koloff would have been pleased. The rainbow seemed almost close enough to touch, but I didn't want to draw attention to myself by reaching out for it.

Shortly before the rainbow, there had been a quick thundershower. It didn't last very long, but its intensity was felt nonetheless. It left puddles that dried quickly in the heat of the Hawaiian sun. Similarly, in our lives, we sometimes go through periods of storm. Though the storms may be short or long, their drops leave puddles of sorrow and despair. We often think the storm will never end. But it always does, and, just like the puddles from the rainstorm, the hurt and scars eventually go away. Long or short, light or intense, we can be assured that whatever we might be currently experiencing is only temporary.

We would all love to have lives that are always joyful and free of any stress or difficulty. But the challenges we endure only cause us to appreciate the happy times even more. Just as no rainbow is ever evident unless it is preceded by a storm, our "up" times would not be valued as much without the requisite and contrasting "down" periods.

Every time I see a rainbow, I remember God's promise to Noah. I believe that God has promises and plans for each of our lives. Sometimes, in the frustration of daily living, we lose sight of those promises. In our state of dissatisfaction, we often lose focus on the reality outside the storm—while it might be raining where we are at that moment, the sun is shining somewhere. We often overlook the blessings we have already received and the knowledge we hold deep in our hearts that trouble is only for a season. Once the storm passes over, there will again be bright sunshine. The rainbow reminds us of how much God cares about us. He has our futures already mapped out, and if we stick to the plans He's laid out, we will come out of the storm with a brighter, more colorful future. However, in order to get to the rainbow periods in our lives, we must first endure the storms.

How precious we must be to receive constant visual reminders of that long-ago promise. Seven colors in the rainbow—seven, the number of completion. Does it get any better?

TRIALS PRECEDE TRANSFORMATION

"All changes, even the most longed for, have their melancholy; for what we leave behind us is a part of ourselves; we must die to one life before we can enter another."

ANATOLE FRANCE

During a recent picnic at Starved Rock, a fat, fuzzy yellow caterpillar began to crawl out of my picnic basket just after I'd closed it. He must've crept onto the top and gotten closed inside. *Yuck,* I thought. *How gross!* I wanted him out of there—and he seemed to want the same thing. The more I thought about it, I was sure he was no happier to be inside my picnic basket than I was to have him there. There he was, crawling along, minding his own business. And, suddenly, he was toppled over and thrust into darkness with no idea where he was. Probably the only thing on his mind was escape—getting out of that dark place and back into the light and the familiar feel of the soft green grass.

I wonder if the caterpillar had any idea where he was as he crawled through the darkness of the picnic basket. He was faced with a difficult circumstance that was not of his own choosing. Was he afraid? Did he know that before too long, light would again appear and he would be able to see his way to wherever he wanted to go? Or did he perhaps think my basket was his cocoon and that he would reside there permanently? One fact about caterpillars is that they molt repeatedly; that is, they go through numerous periods of transformation during their lives. So, my friend the caterpillar was probably fairly used to change.

It seemed that the caterpillar had decided that his present circumstance was temporary and sought to find his way out. By focusing on the light in the distance, visible between the woven slats of the picnic basket, the caterpillar was able to navigate his way out of the basket to reach the light.

Sometimes life topples us into unfamiliar territory, and, like the caterpillar, we stumble around in darkness, trying to find our way back to the light. We encounter periods in our physical, financial, emotional, or spiritual lives when we feel like we have fallen into a dark and scary location that is often not of our own choosing. In our discomfort, we wonder how long we will have to endure this frightening and unfamiliar place. We have no idea which direction to go and sometimes end up going in circles. Yet, just like the caterpillar, if we focus on the light in the distance and make up our minds that our situation is only temporary, we will make it through.

Life is a series of transforming experiences. Although it might have seemed major at the time, what the caterpillar was experiencing was nothing compared to the metamorphosis that awaited it. By now the caterpillar has surely become a butterfly. We all go through life-altering experiences of various intensities that take us from the comfort zones we are currently in, shake us up, toss us around in the dark, and then lead us to a brighter and more promising future. But we can't allow ourselves to get too comfortable once we have "arrived" because another challenge or transformation is on the way. Often, the most trying periods in our lives yield the greatest lessons in personal growth and self-discovery. It is those times that show us what we really have inside.

It's funny. We think of butterflies as beautiful, graceful, enchanting beings. Caterpillars are considered repulsive. Yet they are the very same creature, just at different stages in their life development. Sometimes we look at people in the exact same way. We might see someone who is a single parent, someone who is struggling to pay the bills, someone who is overweight, unkempt, or uneducated. We decide that he or she clearly doesn't have it together. What we fail to realize is that, most likely, this person is in a period of transformation.

Soon, I thought, *that caterpillar will soar over the places where it once crawled. It will grow wings and fly, in view of admiring eyes.* A butterfly seems to be without care as it flits from flower to flower and tree to tree. But in order to become that beautiful butterfly, the caterpillar had to be transformed. Wrapped tightly in a cocoon and unable to move in any direction, it might have seemed that life was over. However, the caterpillar was soon able to release itself from what was keeping it bound. It let go of its old life in order to gain a better life, and we must often do the same. Sometimes we, too, must endure the pain of life-altering circumstances so that we can develop into the butterflies that we are meant to be. To quote Richard Bach, "What the caterpillar calls the end of the world, the master calls a butterfly."

We all go through seasons of difficulty in our lives that we would rather not encounter. If a caterpillar were asked if it would like to go through the painful and frightening experience of being wrapped in a cocoon, in total darkness for a good portion of its life, closed off from the outside world, I'm sure there's a good chance it would choose to remain a caterpillar rather than become a butterfly. But there is a purpose for the pain and uncertainty. Trust the process, and allow the Master to do His work. Just as a caterpillar has no idea that it is going to become a beautiful butterfly, we have no concept of the end result that God is working on in our lives when we go through difficult situations. The fear of financial insecurity, the death of loved ones, the failure of a relationship—it all leaves us feeling as if we are in the dark. Sometimes we think things are fine just the way they are and we'd much rather skip the painful experiences, thank you very much. We resist. We moan. We cry. We say, "Why me?" But God knows the outcome of our journeys. He knows the beautiful creatures that He is developing us into and the rich reward that awaits us at the end of our voyages.

By pushing against the walls of the cocoon in the darkness, the butterfly's wings are getting stronger and it is developing into a new creature. When you're going through a cocoon season in life, you might not see that you have a lot of options. It looks pretty dark and feels very lonely, but you have to push through in order to grow. The familiarity of our own personal cocoons might seem very comfortable. However, if the cocoon is not our final destination, we must understand that the struggle is necessary. We must have the faith to push out of the cocoon, rather than staying in its seeming comfort. We have to break out if we want to be free to soar as the butterflies we were intended to be.

In order for the butterfly to emerge, the caterpillar must be transformed. If you are experiencing the pain of change in your life, don't fight it. Go with it. It might be dark and hazy while in the process of development, but, like that caterpillar, soon you will sprout wings and fly above the clouds into the bright sunshine as the beautiful creature you were designed to be.

LISTEN CLOSELY TO YOUR GPS

"Not till we are lost . . . do we begin to find ourselves."
HENRY DAVID THOREAU

Over the past year and a half, I've been doing some training on the road, that has required a lot of driving. One week alone, I logged 885 miles on my rental car. Although I'd never used it before this project, the navigation system on my smartphone quickly became my new best friend. Even with clear instructions from "Navvie," as I call the voice, I still managed to get lost at times. But Navvie is ever patient with me, simply saying in a sunny voice, "new route" every time I mess up. She never says, "I told you that twice already. What's wrong with you?" She never raises her voice or insults me for making a mistake.

I appreciate her for that, and I try to cooperate as much as possible.

We all have goals we want to achieve—places we see ourselves going in life. Sometimes getting there isn't a straight shot. There are twists and turns along the way, and it's easy to get confused and frustrated when we lose direction. Here are some lessons that Navvie taught me about navigating through life:

- **You must know where you are and where you want to go.** Though uncomfortable with this knowledge at first, I soon became grateful that "the system" always knew where I was at any time. Armed with that knowledge, the only thing I have to tell Navvie is where I am trying to go. In order to achieve our goals, we first have to be honest with ourselves about where we are right now. Then we must have a clear and specific view of where we want to end up. As Stephen Covey says, we have to "start with the end in mind" if we are to reach any of our goals.

- **There is more than one way to get there.** I noticed that when I put an address in the system, Navvie gives me a choice of three routes, with the mileage and estimated travel time for each. I get to choose which route is more appealing to me. I can choose the fastest, the most scenic, and so on. The good thing is that all the routes ultimately lead to my destination. There is always more than one way to arrive at our goals, so we should never get discouraged when our path is not exactly the same as someone else's. Trust that you will eventually arrive at your destination.

- **It is never too late to get back on track.** Sometimes we get stuck in traffic. Other times we need to take a detour. Navvie taught me that it doesn't matter if I get stalled or off track along the way. She doesn't care how long it takes to arrive at our destination. She allows me to pick up right where I left off and keep going. There is no such thing as too late, too old, or too far off to get back on track with your goals. Persistence pays off, and it will always work out in the end, if you just keep moving in the right direction.

- **You might be closer than you think.** One night, I drove around and around within

a half-mile radius, looking for my hotel
for at least 30 minutes. It was right there,
but I couldn't see it because, by design,
it blended in seamlessly with all the other
buildings. (Somehow I'd managed to find a
hotel that was conveniently located right in
the middle of a strip mall, but we won't get
into my shopping habits here.) Sometimes a
goal might seem out of focus. We can't see
it clearly because of everything else going
on around us that distracts us from where
we are heading. If we refocus ourselves, we
just might find that what we want has been
right in front of us all along.

- **Enjoy the journey.** While I navigated
  through unfamiliar territory, I found many
  delightful distractions along the way. From
  historic sites to outlet malls, I took it all in.
  I got the opportunity to visit places that
  I wouldn't have ordinarily seen. I've met
  (well, I've seen) Punxsutawney Phil, the
  supposedly 124-year-old groundhog who
  predicts the weather each February. I've
  visited the Mississippi River town where
  Mark Twain grew up and based his classic
  tales. I've snapped breathtaking pictures of

Yosemite National Park. The list goes on . . . It's important to appreciate where we are on the way to where we're going, even in those moments when we feel "lost." Take some time to stop and smell the roses. It makes the journey more enjoyable, and, before you know it, you will have arrived at your destination.

If your current path isn't taking you where you want to go, it isn't too late to change direction. Don't allow your dreams to die. Get started today! Envision what you want for your life, set your destination, and remember to have fun along the way. And if you need support on your journey, always reach out for guidance.

You Must Prep the Soil

"There are no secrets to success. It is the result of preparation, hard work, and learning from failure."

COLIN POWELL

I don't have a green thumb by any stretch of the imagination. I can take a perfectly healthy houseplant and turn it into a shriveling vine in a matter of months. I blame it on the lack of sunlight—no eastern exposure—but it probably also has to do with the lack of water and food. In fact, I believe that when plants see me coming toward them at Home Depot, they shrink back in fear. "Nooooo! Don't let her buy me! I'll never make it through the year!" Anyway, that is with indoor plants. I fare somewhat better with outdoor plants, probably because God remembers to water them when I forget.

So, every spring, I plant flowers on my "deck." (It is actually a porch, but that is what we call it in my condo association. I think it makes us feel more like homeowners.) I even have a fancy garden set with all the necessary—and some, I think, unnecessary—tools in a nice wicker basket. (I get the spoon and fork, but I still haven't figured out what the straight pokey thing and the bent pokey thing are for.) Once in the garden department, I anguish over selecting just the right varieties and colors of plants. I plan in advance what will go in each individual pot. Don't ask me what I planted in any particular year, because I never remember the names of them past the actual planting. But I'm still proud of my "garden" that explodes in a riot of color every year.

This year, I decided to take a little more care when planting. Instead of just sticking the plants in the pots in the packed-down dirt from last year, I decided to actually till and fertilize the dirt, excuse me, the *soil* (that is the proper term we gardeners use) first. I picked out any remnants from last year's plants, along with any other foreign matter. I sprinkled plant food and worked it through the soil with that thing that looks like a back scratcher, then put on a top layer of potting soil with plant food in it. I paid attention to how much sun was needed for every variety of plant, as well as the spacing needed for each type. Thinking about how my flowers would grow taller and fuller than in previous years got me to thinking about human life.

We are constantly given new chances to grow and achieve in life. Each new year, new job, new house, and new relationship is an opportunity to improve on what we've done in the past. Every new season brings new opportunity. Often we are tempted to just plop the new stuff on top of the old and keep moving. Before embarking on each new chapter in our lives, we should make sure to remove any leftover "scraps" from the old chapter. Any baggage, insecurities, or hurt feelings should be examined and removed. We might need to get rid of some of our old friends. We should also till or "stir up" the ground, making sure our soil has been prepped and fertilized with the proper character traits to receive the new blessings that are headed our way. We need to partake of things that are useful to our mental, physical, and spiritual growth—our sunlight. We should read and listen to uplifting books and tapes and meditate on positive things to stay in the right frame of mind. We also need to watch our "spacing" and not allow ourselves to get too close to people who aren't a positive influence.

In recent years, I embarked on a new chapter in my life, following my lifelong passion for writing. I believe that God has great things in store for me, and for all of us, if we cooperate with His plan. But we have to be willing to put in the extra effort. Skipping any of the steps in the process—tilling, planting, watering—will stunt the growth of any ventures we undertake.

Going through the extra effort when planting my garden wasn't necessarily fun. It took longer than it did before, and I got dirt in my eye. But it was worth the extra effort. I believe that this will be a banner year for my garden and for my life. I hope it is for yours, as well.

DISCOVER YOUR SWEET SPOT

"God gave you . . . [a] zone, a region, a life precinct in which you were made to dwell. He tailored the curves of your life to fit an empty space in His jigsaw puzzle. And life makes sweet sense when you find your spot . . . Stand at the intersection of your affections and successes and find your uniqueness."

MAX LUCADO (EXCERPTED FROM
THE CURE FOR THE COMMON LIFE)

While I'm not an athlete by anyone's standards (Grace is my middle name, but I don't always live up to it), I have played the occasional game of tennis and I know that in most sports, there is a location on the bat, club, racket, or paddle where it is most effective to hit a ball—a "sweet spot." The sweet spot is the site of optimum performance, and it provides the most speed, energy, and power. When hit with the sweet spot, the ball is propelled powerfully forward, with no backward rebound.

As individuals, we also have a sweet spot, where the response to our personal effort is maximized—the intersection of our gifts and passion with the proper opportunities. It is the zone that embodies the best or most effective use of our unique skills and abilities. In other words, it is where we are in our element. I've found that as I'm growing in my purpose, I'm experiencing that sweet spot more and more. It happens sometimes when I'm teaching or coaching or just having a one-on-one conversation with someone. It's when I feel that work is "fun" and when I get positive feedback on what I'm doing. At first it caught me by surprise, and then I realized that is what it is supposed to feel like when you're living in your purpose and using your gifts correctly.

Unfortunately, many people go their entire lives without really understanding or embracing their sweet spots. In case you're still working on identifying yours, here are a few tips to help you clarify it:

- **Utilize your natural gifts.** What skills and capacities do you have? We are all born with at least two or three natural "giftings" that motivate us to our chosen life path. My top giftings are "teacher" and "encourager," followed by "leader." I see those gifts playing out more and more as I begin to live more fully in my purpose. Your unique combination of gifts has been inside of you all along; it's a matter of recognizing those gifts and allowing them to shine. To live in your sweet spot, you must embrace who you are. If your gift is to be a helper, be a helper. If it is to be a leader, stop hiding under someone else's shadow and be the leader you were meant to be.

- **Engage your passion.** Just being good at something isn't enough; you also have to love it. I began college as a chemical engineering major because counselors convinced me that I was good in math and science. The only problem was that I *hated* math and only cared for the experiments in science. I could do math if I had to, but what I really loved was writing and researching topics of interest. Learning new things has always excited me. What excites you? As the question goes, "What would you do for free?"

- **Consider your personality.** No disrespect intended, but I just don't have the personality of a chemical engineer. I'm a people person. I need to be in situations where I'm interacting on a personal level. That is where my energy comes from. Situations that allow for communication and flexibility are where I thrive. Be honest with yourself about what types of activities and environments are the best fits for you.

- **Find ways to engage your sweet spot.** You can do it—whatever "it" is for you—like no one else can, and there are people who need what you have to offer. Your sweet spot will provide for your future. My favorite book says, "A man's gift makes room for him and brings him before great men." Allow your gifts and talents to guide you to the right opportunities. Create your own niche if it doesn't already exist. In times of economic recession, your gift will lead you to opportunities that are the best fit for you, even if you have to create those opportunities yourself. Even using your gift as a hobby or on a volunteer basis is a great place to start. Share it with those around you so that they can also help you to identify opportunities to engage your sweet spot.

In our sweet spot, we experience the most joy and satisfaction in being ourselves. We are able to be content with where we are and what we have. And from that place of peace, pleasure, and joy in just being who we naturally are, energy arises and flows outward to others. And we are able to feel blessed while being a blessing to others. Isn't that what it is all about?

PUSH THROUGH THE CONCRETE

*"Great works are performed,
not by strength, but perseverance."*

SAMUEL JOHNSON

I never cease to be awestruck by God's handiwork. Waves crashing against the shore, trees blowing in the wind, bees pollinating the flowers, dogs playing in the park . . . the balance of nature works perfectly to the smallest detail.

One of my favorite pleasures is to walk along the lakefront in Chicago and then just sit, taking in the beauty of the water and the city on a day when few people are out. I stare at the waves, the trees, the swimmers (human and canine), and our breathtaking downtown skyline, and I simply enjoy being alive. It is at those times I feel closest to God and most at peace with myself. I marvel at all of God's creation. From the smallest blade of grass to the largest skyscraper, He didn't miss a thing. From the insects who maintain the balance of nature to the seaweed-covered rocks jutting up out of the water by the shoreline, it is all awesome to me!

It was on such a day when, reluctantly returning from my walk, I hiked along the rocky shoreline rather than sticking to the bike path. Although there was no other vegetation in that area, I noticed a tiny purple flower growing through a crack in a large concrete slab. Happy for an excuse to tarry, I stopped and looked at this wonder of nature. I thought of how difficult it must have been for that fragile plant to work its way through at least a foot of concrete. What determination! What time it must have taken to complete the process. How did such a delicate object manage such a feat? How did the flower seed even get all the way over there? It seemed almost impossible. Yet there it was for the whole world to see, or at least anyone who cared to notice. No one could look at the flower and say that it couldn't be done.

This visual caused me to think about how easily dissuaded we can become when we have goals in mind but lack the fortitude to see them through. I am quite a bit bigger and stronger than that small flower, but I'm sure that I would've given up the struggle to push through the concrete. The task would have seemed insurmountable and thus not worth the effort. But it was definitely worth the effort, to see that small flower peeking up through the thin crack in the concrete.

What makes the difference between success and mediocrity? Sometimes it is just the willingness to hang in there. Scottish philosopher Thomas Carlyle said, "Permanence, perseverance, and persistence in spite of all obstacles, discouragements, and impossibilities: it is this that in all things distinguishes the strong soul from the weak."

How often do we give up on goals that are difficult yet attainable because we listen to the voice within us that says, "I can't—it isn't possible," instead of the one that tells us that "all things are possible"? If we had the tenacity of that simple flower, there would be no challenge too great for us to overcome. We could achieve our heart's desires. People might wonder how we got such a grand house or impressive car. They might wonder why we are smiling when others are stressed because of difficult economic times. The answer would be that we were persistent despite challenging circumstances.

That little flower basked in the sunlight, totally oblivious to the fact that it was the only flower around. Although it was not in a place where one would typically see a flower, it seemed as if it was right where it belonged. That is how we are when we overcome obstacles to reach our goals. We might not end up where others thought we'd be; we might not even end up where we intended to be. But when we reach the finish line, we'll raise our faces to the sun and realize that we are right where we belong.

MAKE "GREEN" THE NEW BLACK

"Opie, you haven't finished your milk.
We can't put it back in the cow, you know."

AUNT BEE TAYLOR,
THE ANDY GRIFFITH SHOW

Lately, I've been on a crusade to eat from my freezer and cabinets rather than buying more food to stuff in them. It makes sense from the savings, purging, and health perspectives. My friends tease me that my freezer looks as if I have a family of five because it is always stuffed to capacity. One friend dubbed me the "Freezer Queen" because at any time, I can pull leftovers out and have a ready-made dinner. So, as part of my personal "green" campaign, I'm working on depleting what I have before I buy more. I'm trying to employ the same philosophy in the clothing and shoes departments, but that is a much bigger giant to slay. Baby steps.

Always seeing a lesson, I got to thinking . . . what if we "eat" from what we already have in all areas of our lives? What if we thawed out some skills that have been frozen for a while? All of us have at least one talent that could really "feed" someone if we put it to use. Sometimes we don't recognize the gifts that are inside of us because they look small when compared to things other people can do. They might look small to us, but we don't always know the impact that the little things can have on others. Take inventory of what you have to offer that could provide either income opportunities for yourself or opportunities to help someone else. My mother had the gift of mercy, which caused her to enjoy visiting people in nursing homes. That isn't something that most people would think of as world changing, but imagine how much it meant to those she visited. Your gift of cooking or decorating or speaking a kind word might not win you a Nobel Prize or earn you millions of dollars, but it means a lot to those who are on the receiving end.

How much more powerful could we be if, instead of focusing on "more"—instead of wishing for skills, money, or opportunities that we don't have—we just focus on fully utilizing what we already possess? What if we really decided to "live full and die empty"? Imagine the increase in effectiveness, in confidence, and in our impact on the world. If you aren't ready to jump in alone, partner with an organization like the American Cancer Society, Habitat for Humanity, or Faith in Place and volunteer your time and talents to make a difference. If you don't know where to start, check out www.volunteermatch.org or search the Web for local organizations.

Things wasted, whether our food or our gifts and talents, can never be regained. What gifts and talents are you storing in the "freezer" of your life that you haven't thawed out in a while? Go "green" and recycle them! You'll feel better, and you'll inspire others along the way. By the way, my freezer project is coming along quite nicely. I can actually see the sides and back walls! Progress is being made . . .

DON'T BE FROZEN BY FEAR

"The only thing we have to fear is fear itself—nameless, unreasoning, unjustified terror which paralyzes needed efforts to convert retreat into advance."

FRANKLIN DELANO ROOSEVELT

Recently, I worked with motivational speaker Les Brown as the Chicago local director of the Greatness Center. A cross section of people from the city and suburbs attended our empowerment events. Les honored me by allowing me to speak at them. One month, my speech went very well. The next was another story.

It wasn't that I was not prepared. I had rehearsed my speech many times before and was totally ready. And it wasn't that I didn't think my speech was good enough.

I'd tried it out on some friends and associates, and they had assured me it was excellent. The bottom line is that I allowed fear and self-doubt to creep into my mind, and I convinced myself that I shouldn't do my speech that day.

Ironically, my speech was about overcoming obstacles. Included in the speech was a reference to how we can often be our own biggest obstacle, as we allow fear and self-doubt to hold us back from achieving what we know is possible in our lives. Why, then, did I fall victim to it myself? A friend commented recently, "Our greatest lessons are learned through failure." I definitely learned several lessons—about doubting myself, about doubting God, and about allowing opportunities to slip by. And I don't plan to let any of those things happen again. I beat myself up about it for a while (Les said he wished he could help with the beating), but I decided to apply the lessons and move forward full force toward my goals. I'm actually more inspired now to not let any other opportunities pass me by.

How many of your goals and dreams have been aborted because of self-doubt? How much more are you capable of than you actually think? Can you commit to moving forward despite being scared? Whether you are transitioning in your career, starting a new business, or have any other goals that you've been putting on the back burner because of fear, it's time to ramp it up! As long as you have breath, there is still time to accomplish much.

I don't know how my 20-minute presentation would have ranked in the annals of public speaking overall, but it was definitely the greatest speech I never gave.

PAY ATTENTION TO WHAT'S IN FRONT OF YOU

"The moment one gives close attention to anything, even a blade of grass, it becomes a mysterious, awesome, indescribably magnificent world in itself."

HENRY MILLER

I know they say that you're supposed to get rid of anything you haven't worn in six months to a year, but I've never been able to subscribe to that principle. I do part with some pieces throughout the year, but it seems that no matter how many clothes I give away, the closets stay just as full! (I think I see some hands being raised . . .)

When there's too much stuff, you don't always pay attention to what is there. Recently, I ran across a black pantsuit that I hadn't worn in years. It was right at the front end of my main closet, and I see it all the time. For some reason, it never occurred to me to actually pick it up and put it on. Duh! (I wore it the next day and got several compliments.) Made me wonder what other good stuff I am missing out on that is right in front of my face.

How about you? Is there anything (or anyone) in your life that you are taking for granted? What is right in front of you that you might not be seeing clearly?

Are there any obvious career or business opportunities that you might not be taking advantage of? Have you reached out to all your contacts in the past six months to a year? If not, they might be getting a little stale. I decided that it is time to start reaching out to my personal network to explore opportunities for my speaking, training, and coaching. It's said that most millionaires are created in times of economic recession. Why? Because they decide to use the skills and ideas they already have to create opportunities for themselves instead of waiting for times to get better.

What about the people in your life? Sometimes we can neglect relationships that should receive more of our time and attention. In our quest to find happiness, we ignore those who have (or possess the potential to have) the greatest impact on our joy—those who are right in front of us. Do not ignore your key relationships at any cost.

Give them the attention they deserve and they will not only last, but will grow deeper and more fulfilling. In fact, I challenge you to call, right now, someone who has crossed your mind recently but you just haven't taken the time to let them know it.

Even (gasp!) your job or business, while it might be a source of frustration, is often one of the last things you take the time to fully value. Find what attracted you to it in the beginning and relight the spark.

It's time for us to take stock of the things in our lives that we might be ignoring or underappreciating. Take a close look at the front end of your figurative closet, and don't miss out on any more of your good stuff!

WE ARE MORE ALIKE THAN DIFFERENT

"If there's any message to my work, it is ultimately that it's okay to be different, that it's good to be different, that we should question ourselves before we pass judgment on someone who looks different, behaves different, talks different, is a different color."

JOHNNY DEPP

I was standing at the bus stop on a warm spring day, on my way to teach my public speaking classes at Columbia College, when a young man approached me. I could tell right away that he was different. His rumpled dress and the saliva in the corners of his mouth attested to the fact that he did not fit society's standard of "normal."

Of course, like many of us large city dwellers, when approached by a stranger, I wondered, *What is his angle? Is he up to something? Is he going to ask me for money?* But I decided to take a chance and listen to what he had to say.

He came closer to me, folded his hands very formally, and began to speak. "I'd like to tell you a story."

"Okay," I replied, eyeing him warily.

"It was fifteen years ago today," he began. *Okay,* I thought. *Maybe he isn't as young as I thought he was.* He then proceeded, with choppy sentences and phrases, to tell me about a teacher he'd had in high school. It took me a few minutes to get the gist of what he was saying, but I finally gathered that the teacher was mean to him because of his learning disability. She made him feel as if he would never be successful at anything because he was not smart enough. He expressed how what she had said to him those many years ago hurt him. He continued, telling me how the same thing happened to him in junior high with some of his classmates. I tried to encourage him, reminding him that he had gotten through it all. He told me of another experience that was "seven years ago today," and I began to suspect that maybe his timing wasn't exactly accurate.

There was a slight pause in the conversation. Then he asked, "Do you go to church?"

"Yes," I replied.

"Where do you go to church?" I told him the name of my church. "On Stony Island?" he asked, and I nodded.

"I pass by there sometimes."

Slightly surprised at his attention to detail, I asked him, "Where do you go to church?" He told me the name of his church, which I was familiar with. Intrigued, I asked him what activities he was involved in at his church. After stating proudly that he was a "bench member," he listed a few.

"What is your name?" he asked.

"Talayah," I said. "What's yours?"

"Alexis," he said. "You're welcome to come and visit my church." He told me the times of the services, and I invited him to visit my church, as well. He promised he would. We then continued to make small talk—he complimented me on my shoes, asked what brand they were, and so on.

The bus pulled up. Before we boarded, Alexis again turned to me. "Thank you for listening to my story." He held out his hand, and I reached mine out, too.

"Thank you for sharing it with me," I replied. We shook hands and got on the bus.

During the ten-minute ride, Alexis stood next to me and continued to talk. He told me about how he had completed a year at a junior college in Los Angeles. Upon returning to Chicago, he attended another school for a while, but he was not able to complete the program. He went through a job-training program, and, although it took him much longer to finish than the regular schedule, he finally got a job. After a few years, he was let go from the job because he was unable to keep up with the work. Still, he was optimistic that he would get another job. As I listened to him talk, I was struck by his determination and positive outlook, despite his personal challenges.

I thought, *Alexis's story is just like anyone else's.* Although he might be viewed by many as disabled, Alexis was a go-getter. He was determined not to let his obstacles hold him back from achieving his goals. He *would* finish high school. He *would* attend junior college. He *would* get a job. Like many others in our current economy, Alexis is between jobs right now. But he isn't discouraged.

As we approached my stop, he smiled and said, "It was nice meeting you."

"It was nice meeting you, too," I said, smiling back.

He held out his arms for a hug. As I hugged him, he whispered, "I love you."

"I love you, too," I told him, with a warm feeling creeping throughout my being.

I was so touched and inspired by Alexis's story that I started off my first class by talking about him. The lesson plan for that day became centered on the power of sharing personal stories in public speeches.

I'm so thankful that I met Alexis. I would have missed a blessing if I had not taken the time to listen to his story. It warmed my heart and encouraged me with a reminder that we can do anything we put our minds to. We are all more alike than we are different. Sharing our own personal stories encourages others to keep pressing forward to achieve their goals. Be sure to share yours with someone soon. You never know who it might touch.

PERSISTENCE HAS EIGHT LEGS . . .

*"Ambition is the path to success.
Persistence is the vehicle you arrive in."*

BILL BRADLEY

One day I realized that I had an intruder. He wasn't invited, nor was he welcome. But he certainly was persistent. We could all learn a lot from the spider who decided to make my car his home. I'm sure it was the same spider, because no matter where I went, city or suburbs, no matter where I parked my car, I was sure to come out and find a spiderweb on my driver's side mirror. No matter how many times the wind blew the web away or I wiped it away, it always reappeared in the same spot. I was beginning to wonder whose car it really was!

Although I didn't appreciate it in the spider, persistence is usually an admirable quality and one that I'm striving to make a habit. It is very easy to get discouraged when life deals us a difficult blow. Sometimes the "webs" we have carefully and painstakingly constructed do get knocked down. In a period of double-digit unemployment, wavering stock prices, and record home foreclosures, it is easy to get discouraged and lose focus of our goals. We have to learn to persevere despite the challenges we might face.

Here are some other things I've learned about persistence:

- **Current circumstances are not the best indicators of future success.** A lean bank account today does not preclude you from having wealth in your future. Persistence and a positive attitude will help you get over the hurdles that block your path to success. Just "hanging in there" will sometimes get us far. Just like the tide, there will be ebbs and flows in your circumstances. If you put forth your best effort during the difficult times, your successes will be that much sweeter.

- **Successful people often fail their way to success.** Mark Victor Hansen and Jack Canfield's first Chicken Soup book was turned down by 144 publishers. They now have over 200 Chicken Soup titles in print and translations into more than 40 languages. Mark Victor Hansen is one of the most prolific authors in the world, with over 150 million books sold. What if he'd given up after publisher number 144 instead of trying one more time? At the beginning of his career, Tom Cruise was told that he wasn't attractive enough to be an actor. His persistence led to becoming one of the highest-paid actors in Hollywood. The worst thing that can happen isn't failing. The worst thing that can happen is *giving up.*

- **Defeat is only temporary.** "Impossible" is just a state of mind. Breakthroughs happen every day; it's just a matter of hanging in there until yours arrives. While giving up is certainly an option, how would you feel if you gave up, only to realize your obstacle was removed the next day? Stay the course until the wind shifts the sails.

When you are working on any major goal, your level of motivation will naturally increase and decrease depending on what is going on in your life—other obligations, health issues, stress, and so on. Persistence is the determination to keep moving forward regardless of outside forces. Clarity of vision leads to dedicated action; keeping your goals at the forefront of your mind with a visual list or even a vision board is a great way to stay focused.

Most meaningful endeavors have challenges. Whether your focus is your career or business, physical fitness, finances, or any other life area, it is only those who persevere until the end who will reap the rewards. Don't give up on your purpose or your goals.

It was Calvin Coolidge who said, "Nothing in the world can take the place of persistence. Talent will not; nothing is more common than unsuccessful people with talent. Genius will not; unrewarded genius is almost a proverb. Education will not; the world is full of educated derelicts. Persistence and determination alone are omnipotent. The slogan 'press on' has solved and always will solve the problems of the human race." So keep pressing on. Only the strong survive!

FIND YOUR "WHY"

*"There are two great days in a person's life—the day
we are born and the day we discover why."*

WILLIAM BARCLAY

What is your personal "why"? For what reason are you on this earth? What drives and motivates you to success? This is such an important question, but it is one few ever answer. Most people go through their entire lives without understanding their true motivations. Some spend their time chasing money. Some spend it chasing love and relationships. Some spend it seeking a "high" through food, alcohol, or drugs. When we focus on such superficial things, we always end up feeling frustrated and discontented. There has to be a deeper longing that motivates us. What is really at the core of our being? What is it that will truly make us fulfilled?

It took me awhile to figure out my "why," but now that I have, it all fits. In addition to writing and empowering others through my teaching and speaking, I am absolutely in *love* with flexibility and creativity! I adore not having to go to a nine-to-five job every day. I love being able to control my time and work when and where I want. My battery gets charged by interacting with all the new people I meet. I love to travel and explore other cultures. Some of my friends and family members say that they still don't know what I do. But everything I do in my professional life fits within the boundaries of what I'm passionate about. I teach on the college level, I train, I coach, I speak, and I facilitate the workshops that I create. I hosted a radio show (is there television in my future?). I even get to travel quite a bit at the expense of others. All of these activities fit my personal "why," and I've never been happier at any time in my life than I am right now.

Your "why" has to be big enough to motivate you to success, no matter what. If you look back at any goals you didn't achieve in your life, there's a good chance the reason was that your "why" wasn't big enough. If you truly understand your "why," the "how" part of it won't matter. As long as you are putting all your energy and focus into why you are here—your unique purpose—the how will take care of itself. Your confidence comes from knowing that you will succeed at your why.

Think about it. If you are a parent, what motivates you to be a successful parent? Is it the goodwill you'll receive from others when they see what a great job you did with your children? Is it because your children are beautiful and well behaved? Is it that you love cleaning up all the messes they make, from soiled diapers to damaged fenders on cars? No. Your motivation is love. You give your best to your child—you always have and you always will, no matter what it takes—because of love. You are compelled by love, no matter how bad the child might act and no matter how old the child might be.

We are having so many issues with border patrol in America right now, because there are people who would risk life and limb just to be here. We hear stories of people braving shark-infested waters, riding on the underbellies of trucks, and so on, because they are so committed to having the life they dream about. What would you be willing to swim through shark-infested waters to gain?

What motivates you in your business? In your job? Working just for a paycheck is never enough. What motivates you regarding your health? In your relationships? Why do you give your time and money to a certain charity? Whatever major goals you set should have a strong "why" that will motivate you to successfully complete them. If there isn't something that constantly pulls at your core in one of your major goals, you will not give your all to that goal.

I never tried to figure out how I would get into any of the roles that I'm now in. They all came into my path as I moved forward in my purpose. I'm not worried about the "how" for the future. I'm just going to keep living my passion and doing what I love, and welcome the opportunities as they come.

If you are not fully committed to your goals, whether they are business goals, personal goals, or volunteer activities, you will not give them the attention they deserve. If you see that happening in any area of your life, take a step back and reevaluate your "why" when it comes to that activity. If the "why" isn't strong enough, maybe you should shift your focus to just those activities that are truly important to you. It is better to be a success at what you're passionate about than to be mediocre at what others view as being important.

LESSON #15

FOCUS IS THE
KEY TO SUCCESS

"If you chase two rabbits, both will escape."

UNKNOWN

A friend recently told me the secret to training a lion (sorry, Siegfried and Roy). It's all about focus. How can the lion tamer control the massive beast with just a small chair? It's because the chair has three legs. The lion is confused by three prongs coming at him at once and doesn't know which leg of the chair to attack, so it does nothing. It can't focus on all three legs at the same time.

Recently, I got a strong lesson on the importance of focus. I'm the queen of multitasking and have always believed that I could juggle two or three things at once—talking on the phone, typing an e-mail, watching the news, and so on. I'm coming to the realization that if you're doing multiple things at once, you're really not doing any of them optimally. This point was driven home for me when I was out shopping during a recent staycation. I was in one of my favorite discount stores, shopping and talking on the phone. I picked out a $14.99 top and some "unmention-ables" and carried them in my hand as I continued to shop and talk to a friend on the phone. Deciding that there was nothing that I was really interested in purchasing, I walked out of the store, through the parking lot, then opened my car door, and got in the driver's seat. Then I noticed that something felt strange. Why was I doing everything with one hand? I realized that I had inadvertently shifted the clothes to the same hand that was holding my phone. It was because I still had the unpaid merchandise in my other hand! Yes, I went back and paid for it (in case you were wondering). Luckily, I was not arrested, but I learned a valuable lesson nonetheless: focus is crucial. I thought I was power shopping. I thought I was being attentive to my friend on the phone. The truth is I was not truly pay-ing attention to anything that I was doing. Not only was I not focused on my shopping, but I was not giving my full attention to the telephone conversation, either. I was not being fair to the person who was on the other end of the line. An unknown person once said, "The first rule of focus is this: wherever you are, be there."

We all have numerous demands on our time and attention. People will always try to pull us into whatever they are involved in. Even as I write this story, I'm being distracted by e-mails, texts, and so on. It is easy to lose focus, especially when the things pulling at us are enjoyable (I really could appreciate a good game of Spider Solitaire right now), but there is a time and place for everything. When we have goals we want to achieve, it is time to focus.

The other day, I was asked by a woman I'd met through business networking how I am able to juggle different pursuits and maintain my focus. I admit that at one point, because my interests are so varied, I allowed myself to be distracted by the number of options that were constantly being presented to me. But, as I explained to the woman, my business coach once told me that whatever I consider getting involved in needs to fit at least 80 percent of my personal mission. Keeping that in mind has allowed me to focus on the activities that support my overall passions and goals and to say no to the activities that would derail me. By saying no to the things that lead you away from your purpose, you can say yes to the things that enhance it.

Here are some tips that will help you to be more focused in your daily activities:

- **Write it down.** Make a list of the tasks that will get you to your goal. Regularly update your list of repetitive and nonrepetitive tasks. Repetitive tasks are those things you need to do every day—check e-mail, make five sales calls. These only need to be updated if any no longer apply and/or new ones should be added. Nonrepetitive tasks are those that change from day to day—pick up a new printer cartridge, update your resumé. It is good to plan these out at the beginning of each week, for the entire week, assigning a day and time for each task. New tasks can be added as the need arises. Not only will this keep you focused and minimize distractions, but it will give you a sense of accomplishment as you check off each completed task.

- **Turn it off!** The radio, the television, the phone, text messages, e-mail—all are activities that can suck up our time and leave us wondering how the day passed so quickly without our getting things done. Have designated hours when you turn off the distracters so that you can focus on what (or who) is most important.

- **Eliminate clutter.** It is difficult to concentrate in a messy environment. So, to keep your brain clear, keep your work area free of clutter. ("Physician, heal thyself.")

- **Take regular breaks.** Take a stretch break (not a food break) to relax and rejuvenate your body and mind. If the weather is nice, reward yourself for completing a task with a short walk outside.

- **Visualize the end result.** See the mental picture of your goal being achieved. Visualize what will happen when you get there—how you will feel, what you will do, and who will be with you to celebrate when you have reached your goal. Your subconscious mind can't tell the difference between what you believe is happening and what is really happening, so allow yourself a moment to feel the joy of already having achieved your goal.

- **Make yourself accountable.** Get a coach or an accountability partner or join a Mastermind group (we'll learn more about them later on in the book). Share your goals with others who will hold you accountable to complete the tasks you have committed to.

- **Get moving.** Exercise will get the blood flowing to your brain (not to mention the rest of your body) and increase your creativity and focus. So, take an exercise break at some point during the day to rev up your engine.

- **Get some rest**. Getting adequate rest allows your brain and body to function at a higher capacity so that you will be more focused the next day.

You will see powerful results in your life when you get into the habit of creating focus in whatever you're doing. If you're working from home, turn off the television or radio and focus on your work. If you're talking to a client on the phone, step away from your e-mail while you're on the call. Give your complete attention to whatever task you're undertaking and eliminate distractions. Resist the urge to multitask and you'll do everything just a little bit better.

Tony Robbins said, "Most people have no idea of the giant capacity we can immediately command when we focus all of our resources on mastering a single area of our lives." Stay focused on your goals. I'd love to hear about your progress!

LESSON #16

YOU ARE
YOUR ENERGY

*"We don't see the things the way they are.
We see things the way we are."*

TALMUD

Have you ever been impacted by negative energy from another person? Or transferred your own energy to someone else? We have to be mindful at all times of what we are projecting to others. I was reminded of that lesson not long ago.

At an event, I ran into a woman I hadn't seen in years. It was great to see her, as we'd always had great rapport. As soon as we started talking, I made a sarcastic comment that I meant as a joke. The joke fell very flat, and it wound up sounding negative and complaining. I could tell from the look on her face that she was taken aback (open mouth, insert foot). I was so embarrassed that I slinked off without explaining myself. I tried to contact her afterward, but she never responded.

To this day, I feel bad about the negative energy I projected in that moment. As I traced it back, I realized that it had stemmed from a conversation I'd just finished with another person, where we were discussing how tough things had become economically. I'd transferred that negative energy to the next person I spoke with even though I thought I was making a joke. I understood then that we don't always realize how deeply negative thoughts affect us. We think that making small talk about how bad the economy is or how tough it is to get business is just lightweight banter, but it can really take root and grow inside of us if we aren't careful. We should thoroughly weigh our words before releasing them to others.

Here are a few tips to stay positive during the storms, so that you don't transfer negative energy to others:

- **Take a break from the news.** Negativity in the media has a huge subconscious impact. Be careful of overconsumption of news shows. Try reading just the headlines of articles to get an idea of the story, and be selective about reading the details. And definitely stay away from the blog comments at the end of online articles.

Many of these are written by Internet trolls who just want to incite an argument. Nothing good can come from soaking in everyone else's opinions.

- **Watch uplifting shows and read positive books.** I don't watch much TV, but one Saturday—all day long, I'm embarrassed to admit—I felt like vegging. Talking to a friend on the phone a few hours in, I confessed that I was feeling kind of down. He said, "You must be watching . . ." (not calling any names). And I was! I started laughing because it dawned on me that sitting there, watching show after show of people cheating on each other, killing their spouses, and so on, had impacted my attitude. Be careful of what your brain ingests.

- **Engage in positive conversations.** Avoid lengthy conversations with people who constantly complain or gossip. Not only is it a waste of time, but you might absorb some of their negative energy.

Negativity projected can never be recalled; you can't put the toothpaste back in the tube. Our "green" movement should include purging ourselves of negative thoughts and statements, as well as eliminating waste.

We must be careful of what we feed our minds, the thoughts we entertain, and the conversations we have. The way we choose to be at any particular moment is what we project to others in that moment. So, let's create some positive energy!

ASK YOURSELF: WHAT AM I SETTLING FOR?

"There is no passion to be found playing small—in settling for a life that is less than the one you are capable of living."

NELSON MANDELA

Last year, I took a friend out for a birthday celebration and we got into a debate about which was better, lobster or crab. I readily admitted that although I like crab legs better, I'd ordered the lobster because it was easier to eat. I didn't feel like putting in the work to crack open the crab legs. That got me thinking. How many things are we settling for in our lives because they are easier to obtain than what we really want for ourselves?

Are we staying in a career that doesn't allow us to fully use our gifts because of fear or lack of motivation? Are we settling for unfulfilling relationships because we don't want to put in the work it takes to create and/or maintain a strong one? Is it easier to just accept what is available rather than wait for what is the best fit? Are we allowing weight or health issues to remain because we don't want to put in the effort to exercise and/or prepare healthy meals?

I was cooking the other day (happens every now and then) and decided to try my hand at some new dishes. I put a lot of effort into those unfamiliar dishes, and they came out pretty tasty. The one thing that I didn't give much attention to was a dish that I was used to cooking. And guess what? The familiar dish was the worst one. That showed me that we can't take the routine things in our lives for granted. We have to put our best effort into everything that we want to turn out well.

Substandard effort yields substandard results. Are there any areas of your life where you're not playing full out? Is it your health? Your finances? Your career or business? Your relationships? Are you settling for less than you want or deserve in any area of your life?

There is no time like the present to create new habits that will get us where we really want to be in life instead of settling for less. Once those habits are created, we can put systems in place to support them. Here are a few steps to get you started:

- **Embrace your "why."** Remember what I said about finding your "why"? Think about what motivates and drives you. What are you passionate about? What do you do better than anyone else you know? Your passion is always tied to your purpose, your "why." Figure out what you really want, what makes you feel fulfilled, and what feels natural to you. If you don't know what you want, anything will do. What do you really want in your career or business, your relationships, your health, your finances, your spirituality? You can even have smaller "whys" for minor goals—if your motivation is to lose two pounds this week, will that chocolate bar on the table really serve that purpose?

- **Know your value and purpose.** We are each born with specific gifts and abilities, along with a unique personality and thinking style that determines how we are wired. When we lack understanding of our unique value and try to struggle to be like someone else, we become frustrated and unhappy. It is only when we allow our passion and purpose to drive our actions that we find fulfillment in our lives and our work. We don't have to compare ourselves to anyone else; we just have to be the best at who we already are.

- **Stop waiting for the perfect time.** I don't know about you, but I've never seen "Someday" written on a calendar. Get busy now! As the saying goes, "Nothing works unless you do." It's time to play a bigger game. The human anatomy was not designed to straddle a fence. It hurts. Get off the fence and go after your big dream. It doesn't have to be perfect; it just has to get done. You can make it better later.

- **Be willing to do the work.** Life is hard, and nothing of value is ever handed to us. Pain and discomfort are part of the process. I recently heard someone say that we shouldn't feel entitled to anything we didn't sweat and struggle for. The struggle is what builds muscle. Whatever it is that you truly want—a job, a business, a relationship, a svelte figure, money in the bank—you have to work for it. The same rules apply in every area of life. Push past the fear, stop using the distractions as excuses, and roll up your sleeves.

- **Get some support.** Utilize books and courses that will motivate you and help you to expand your knowledge base. Build your team. You don't have to do it alone. You can get a coach, a mentor, or an accountability partner, or you can even form a Mastermind group of people who you trust. Surround yourself with people who will give you honest, relevant feedback (I stress relevant, because not everyone is qualified to speak to your situation). Others can see things in your situation that you might not see and can provide valuable insight that can move you along your desired path more quickly. Be sure to also add people to your network who are already where you want to be. It will force you to play a bigger game. And remember to reach back to those whom you can help.

Go for your goals, and don't settle for second best. Next time, I'll have the crab legs.

CHOOSE YOUR BLOCKS CAREFULLY

"Many of life's failures are people who did not realize how close they were to success when they gave up."

THOMAS ALVA EDISON

Did you ever play with blocks as a child? What did you build? Perhaps you built a one-room house. Maybe you built a wall or a fort to protect yourself from enemy attack. Blocks are useful tools for developing creativity and thinking outside the box. But sometimes certain blocks can hold us back.

By definition, a block is a solid, rectangular building unit. However, a block can also be defined as an obstruction that impedes passage or progress. There is definitely more than one kind of block. There are physical blocks, and there are the blocks we carry in our minds that prevent us from reaching our full potential. These are the things that obstruct our view of reality. These are the things that we sometimes cannot get over or around as we try to achieve our goals. Often, we become frustrated and doubt our own abilities because of these mental blocks.

My grandfather lived with us in his later years until he died at the age of 102. He had one major goal during that time. Like most older people, he longed for the familiarity of home. Unfortunately, his home was in rural Arkansas, on a 100-acre farm that was over 800 miles away, and there was no one there to care for him. Having a "senior" mind, he convinced himself that he could easily walk home, and he tried on several occasions. Many were the times that we would divide up and scour the neighborhood looking for him or, even scarier, have some stranger show up with him on our doorstep, demanding money because my grandfather had promised to pay him or her to take him home (of course, he meant home to Arkansas, not to our house in Chicago). Finally, convinced that he could not walk the entire way, he learned the way to the Greyhound bus station, about five blocks from the house, and would walk there and ask to be put on a bus to Arkansas.

My mom adjusted to his changing ways and learned to lock the doors and remove the keys, so that he couldn't get out. He loved to sit outside during the summer, so she would unlock the back door so that he could relax in the yard. To keep him from going out of the yard, she would lock both gates.

One evening at dusk, she went out to bring my grandfather back into the house for dinner. She couldn't find him at first. When she finally did, he was crouched down, hiding behind a large evergreen tree by the garage. She asked him why he was there, and he laughed sheepishly and explained.

He was waiting until dark to make his "escape." Earlier, he'd spotted two large concrete blocks in our next-door neighbor's yard. He'd climbed the fence into the neighbor's yard to get the blocks. He'd placed one block on either side of the fence—my grandfather was a very strong man, even in his late 90s—and climbed back over the fence into our yard to hide and wait until nightfall. The plan was that he would then climb the fence, with the aid of the blocks, and leave through the neighbor's gate.

Now, there was just one small flaw in my grandfather's logic. Did you pick up on what it was? Let's review: he climbed the fence to get the blocks that he needed to enable himself to climb the fence. Did he really need the blocks to climb the fence or did he just convince himself that he needed the blocks to climb the fence? It never occurred to him that if he had already climbed the fence without the aid of the blocks, he didn't really need them. In this case, we were dealing not just with physical blocks, but with mental blocks, as well.

Sometimes we have our own mental blocks that we have picked up along life's journey. We convince ourselves that we cannot operate with just what we have. We think we need to be smarter, richer, better looking, better positioned, and so on, in order to be successful in life. But we have all that we need to succeed already in us. When Moses doubted his ability to lead the people out of Egypt, God told him to use what he already had in his hand. The same goes for us. If we make the most of the skills and talents that we already have, we can achieve whatever success we desire.

Most people have so much more potential than they will ever fully utilize. Earl Nightingale said, "We can let circumstances rule us, or we can take charge and rule our lives from within." Let's remove the mental blocks and utilize the building blocks we already possess to achieve our full potential.

NATURE AND NURTURE—WE ALL PLAY A PART

"Genes and family may determine the foundation of the house, but time and place determine its form."

JEROME KAGAN, PROFESSOR OF
DEVELOPMENTAL PSYCHOLOGY

Anyone who has visited Chicago, especially during winter, has probably encountered "The Hawk." The Hawk describes the blustery air currents that gave Chicago its much-deserved nickname, the "Windy City." There is another explanation for the name that involves loquacious politicians (aka "air bags"), but we'll stick with the weather analogy for the purposes of this narrative.

Each spring, when walking along the lakefront, I marvel at the improvements that are being made to beautify our city. Every year, there are more trees planted, better landscaping, a brand-new observation area or park, and so forth. Even our former third airport, Meigs Field, has been turned into a park with a concert venue. While out walking one morning and admiring the landscape, I noticed something different about the smaller trees. Most of the newly planted saplings had three iron stakes in the ground around them that were attached to them by strong wire cords. The stakes and cords served to prop up and protect the trees from those gusty winds that Chicago is famous for, so that they would grow straight and strong. Nature allowed the trees to grow, but they had to be nurtured to grow in the right direction, and they had to be protected from anything that might cause harm.

When I saw how those young trees were bolstered against the wind, it reminded me of how we need to support and care for the youth in our society. Those of us who are already developed should nurture and protect them from the elements so that they can safely grow to maturity. Without guidance from someone who has traveled the path to maturity, they can easily grow in the wrong direction.

On that same walk, I noticed that only one variety of semimature maple trees was protected in the same manner as the young saplings with the stakes and cords. It dawned on me that it is not just the young who need support, but anyone who is physically, emotionally, or spiritually weak. We see so many people every day, especially in urban areas, who are unemployed, physically or mentally impaired, emotionally scarred, or suffering from addictions, that we often become jaded. We walk right past them without giving a thought to their needs. Many times, we are cynical because there are so many scam artists who try to play on the sympathies of the public to make ends meet, rather than doing it the old-fashioned way—by working. Sometimes we may even poke fun at those who have any of the aforementioned issues. In these tough economic times, more people are in need. And, often, these are the times when we might focus more on our own needs than on the needs of others. What we should do is pray for those who are in trouble, ask God to direct us to those who need our help, and thank Him that He has blessed us with sight, hearing, a sound mind, gainful employment, and so on.

In the wake of so many recent tragedies—terrorist attacks, wars, mass shootings, tsunamis, hurricanes, and other natural disasters—this is brought even more to the forefront of our minds. I remember my grandfather praying, in his hoarse, raspy voice, that God would "bless all those that it is my duty to pray for" and thanking Him "that things are as well with me as they are." When we are thankful for the things that God has done in our lives, we can then open up our hearts to others and personally demonstrate God's love to them. So, why not ask God today to show you someone who is in need of your special love, gifts, and talents? You might be led to do something as major as adopting a child or as minor as volunteering at a homeless shelter. But whatever you do to give back, know that you will make a difference in someone's life. And also know that *your* life will be greatly enriched in the process.

USE IT OR LOSE IT

"Use it or lose it."

JIMMY CONNORS

We are all blessed with natural ability in some form. Each of us has a knack for something. It might be musical aptitude, analytical thinking, a persuasive personality, the gift of gab, or countless other skills. More often than not, our capabilities are never fully utilized. Sometimes this is because we are thrust into the midst of family or other obligations that take precedence in our lives. At other times, it is because our gifts have not been recognized by us or by others and are therefore untapped. Unfortunately, it is often a lack of focus or even just plain laziness that keeps us from utilizing our faculties to their fullest. Whatever the reason, it is never too late to stir up our gifts and use them to impact the lives of others.

Recently, I had a flat tire and went to a service station to have it repaired. The attendant plugged my tire and told me I needed to have not only that tire but all four of my tires replaced because dry rot had set in. It was just a matter of time, he said, before they'd blow out on me. Dry rot in a tire? I'd never heard of that! He asked how much I drove my car. I always astound people when I mention my mileage. I typically average 6,000 miles per year, about half the average of a typical driver. You'd think that would preserve the life of the car and increase its resale value. Not so. So much for the "little old lady who only drove to church" theory. The tires on my car had dry rotted because of low usage. My previous car had transmission problems because of low usage. I could go on . . . My garbage disposal stopped working because of lack of use; my gas fireplace stopped working because of—you guessed it—lack of use. Even the muscles in your body will atrophy if you do not use them. Just like these physical items, our gifts and talents can "dry rot" if we don't use them.

Think of how much better off the world would be if everyone in it operated to their full capacity in every area of life. What if every person with the intelligence of Albert Einstein, the creativity of Pablo Picasso, the musical ability of Wolfgang Amadeus Mozart, or the determination of Helen Keller used all of his or her talents to their fullest? Take just a minute and think about it.

When you rent a car and prepay for a full tank of gas, I'm sure you don't take the car back half full. Don't you want to drive out the full tank? You're paying for it anyway. You might as well make that extra trip to the mall or the forest preserve. The same theory applies to your life and talents. How much more fulfilling it would be to finish your life on empty than to leave gas in your tank. When you leave this earth, there should be no untapped potential left in you. You should have used every gift and talent you were blessed with. You, much like the rental car, should be on "E."

So, shine up that old violin, dust off the tap shoes, tune up the piano, or warm up those vocal chords—it is time to get serious about using your gifts. Remember that while you still have life in you, it is never too late to resurrect those old talents, polish them up, and get to work. Both you and the world will be better off for it.

DECLARE YOUR INDEPENDENCE

"If money is your hope for independence you will never have it. The only real security that a man can have in this world is a reserve of knowledge, experience, and ability."

HENRY FORD, AMERICAN INDUSTRIALIST

Independence Day occurs during the month of July, accompanied by all the requisite traditions: picnics, BBQs, parades, and, of course, fireworks. The date typically celebrates our country's independence, but what does independence mean to you on a personal level? Is it financial freedom? Fulfillment in your business or career? The freedom to manage your own time? Satisfying and productive relationships? Being more spiritually connected? Enjoying better health?

Although I have always admired entrepreneurs, I was never brave enough to leave the cushion of my corporate job to join the ranks of the self-employed. That is, until I was downsized. After three mergers, enough was enough for me anyway. Instead of being upset about it, I looked at it as an opportunity to do what I'd been longing to do for years. For me, independence is being able to do what I truly love and having a flexible schedule. There is something to be said for steady corporate paychecks, but, for me, the trade-off is definitely not worth it. I believe that following my passion will create all the paychecks I need.

Our society attaches a lot of significance to fame and fortune. It is easy to get pulled into a mentality that is overly focused on material things only to realize that those things are not the source of true happiness and fulfillment. We should keep our focus on what is really important to us, including the special people in our lives.

Step back and reevaluate what is really important to you and where you want life to take you. Think about what fulfillment means to you. Forget about what society or those around you say you should strive for, and think about what you really want. Often, people are so busy chasing money or relationships, seeking temporary satisfaction, or collecting more "stuff" that they miss out on what really matters. As long as you are still breathing, it is never too late to start over and create a new vision for your life. (If I did it, you can, too!)

Declare this time as your time of personal liberation. Free yourself from whatever is holding you back from achieving your life vision. Liberate your mind from negative self-talk, and believe that you can accomplish whatever goal you set out to achieve. Unshackle yourself from any toxic relationships that weigh you down and dampen your spirit. Let go of all excuses. Unbind your creativity, and think outside your present circumstances. Release your inner child who believes that anything is possible. Whatever it is that is holding you back, unchain it and be free!

We all have goals we want to achieve, but it isn't always clear how to bridge the gap between where we are and where we want to go. How do we get there in our finances, in our health, in our spiritual walk, and so on? Author, educator, and clergyman Henry van Dyke said, "In the progress of personality, first comes a declaration of independence, then a recognition of interdependence." As strange as it might sound, achieving independence requires that we have a support system. Coaches, accountability partners, support groups—we all need someone to help us on our life's journey. So don't be afraid to reach out whenever you need it.

Here's an exercise to get you started: Brew a cup of tea. Write down one limiting belief that you have about any one area of your life. Examine why that statement is not true for you. Rewrite the statement to create a powerful and liberating declaration that affirms what you are capable of achieving and *will* achieve in that life area. And you can share these statements with others on Twitter or Facebook, using the hashtag #LightBulbMoments. I'd love to hear them, too; you can send your favorite ones to me @talayahstovall or post them on my Facebook page. Here's to your personal independence!

LIGHTEN YOUR LOAD

"The mark of a successful man is one that has spent an entire day on the bank of a river without feeling guilty about it."

UNKNOWN

Opening my e-mail one day, I came across a story that goes like this: A lecturer was trying to explain stress management to an audience. He raised a glass of water and asked, "How heavy is this glass of water?" People called out answers ranging from 2 ounces to 18 ounces. The lecturer replied, "The absolute weight doesn't really matter. It depends on how long you try to hold it.

"If I hold it for a minute, that's not a problem. If I hold it for an hour, I'll have an ache in my arm. If I hold it for a day, you'll have to call an ambulance. In each case, it's the same weight, but the longer I hold it, the heavier it becomes.

"And that's the way it is with stress management," he continued. "If we carry our burdens all the time, sooner or later, as the burden becomes increasingly heavy, we won't be able to carry on. As with the glass of water, you have to put it down for a while and rest before holding it again. When we're refreshed, we can carry on with the burden.

"So, before you return home tonight, put the burden of work down. Don't carry it home. You can pick it up tomorrow. Whatever burdens you're carrying now, let them down for a moment if you can. Relax; pick them up later after you've rested. Life is short. Enjoy it!"

I don't know who to credit with this story—it's featured on many websites, blogs, and e-mails. But isn't it the truth? Carrying excess "baggage" in our lives can weigh us down. We need to learn how to handle the bags. When performing physical exercise, you can't get buff all at once. We're advised to lift weights, then give our muscles 48 hours to recuperate before lifting again. The stress and strain breaks down the fibers of our muscles. However, at the end of a rest period, they will have regenerated and will be stronger than before. At that time, we can pick up the weights again.

What happens, though, when the burdens are too heavy for us to lift at all? That is when we have to ask for assistance. That assistance could come through a gentle nudging in our spirit or in the form of a person who crosses our path at just the right time. Whichever the case might be, we must learn not to let ourselves get stressed about whatever it is that we are carrying. We should relax and wait for guidance on how to proceed.

How do you deal with the burdens in your life? Do you hold on to them until they make you physically ill? Do you treat everything as an emergency? Do you take out your stress on those around you? Or do you "let go and let God"?

There is a Chinese proverb that says, "Tension is who you think you should be. Relaxation is who you are." When we let go of all of life's "shoulds" and "coulds" and accept and embrace the journey we're on, we will see a decrease in the level of stress in our lives and an increase in peace.

We all go through times when life is not exactly as we would have hoped or planned, but we can be confident that even the worst of times are only temporary and things will get better. A truly happy person is one who can enjoy the scenery on a detour.

MAKE SURE THE INSIDE MATCHES . . .

"People are like stained-glass windows. They sparkle and shine when the sun is out, but when the darkness sets in their true beauty is revealed only if there is a light within."

ELISABETH KÜBLER-ROSS

Have you ever bitten into a shiny, juicy-looking apple and found that it was mushy and brown on the inside? How disappointing is that? Would you rather have an apple that is highly polished on the outside or one that is crisp, sweet, and tasty on the inside?

I have a friend who actually sees people as they are inside. She takes in their behaviors and personalities and determines whether they are attractive or unattractive.

Often her assessment of beauty (or the lack thereof) doesn't match the assessment the rest of us would make with our physical eyes. We have to remind ourselves that there's a person *within* the one we're talking to. My friend is not looking at the container; she's looking at the contents. Not a bad way to be.

I often have the opportunity to participate in women's events, and I love to see ladies enjoying and pampering themselves. It is wonderful to treat ourselves from time to time and make ourselves feel special. But I've noticed that many times so much more emphasis is put on what we're decorating ourselves with on the outside and not what we're putting on the inside. Now, I love clothes, shoes, and jewelry as much as (okay, who am I kidding—*more than*) the next girl. But I believe it is important for all of us—and I'm talking to you guys, as well—to build up the inside and invest in things that are going to make a difference in our lives, long term.

I stopped by a great event recently. The women were getting pedicures and all kinds of spa treatments and they were buying makeup, jewelry, and purses from the vendors. (I wish I could've stayed!) The event hall was completely packed, and there was a line down the block just to get inside. And, get this—the event wasn't scheduled to start for another ten minutes! They had to open the doors ahead of time because everyone showed up early.

What if we had that same enthusiasm in other areas? How powerful could we grow to be if we lined up at a library or a bookstore?

Sadly, the nail polish will chip and the shoes will go out of style. But when we invest in our own personal and professional growth and development, that will take us to the next level in our careers, businesses, spirituality, relationships, health, finances, or any other life area. Let's expand our minds and our networks by reading constructive books, attending empowering conferences, and networking with positive and growth-oriented people. Let's set aside some of our resources—time, money, and talent—to invest in what will really impact our futures, not just in what shines us up on the outside. Building a powerful presence on the inside as well as the outside is a winning combination!

LIFE LESSONS FROM THE TEMPTATIONS

*"The difference between school and life?
In school, you're taught a lesson and then given a test.
In life, you're given a test that teaches you a lesson."*

TOM BODETT

I have two older brothers, so I remember hearing a lot of Motown music growing up. One of our favorite groups was the Temptations. Known for their distinct harmony and finely tuned choreography, they became the definitive male vocal group of the 1960s and early 1970s. Their music is *timeless* and has inspired multiple generations. I was watching the Temptations movie recently—mostly just to hear the music—but I actually learned a few lessons as I watched the story unfold. The group went through numerous transitions before they ended up with their final roster of members. Those who stayed the course—who didn't give up, regardless of obstacles—became successful in their music careers. But not everyone stayed the course. While you read, see if you can figure out which group member is being referred to.

Here are the lessons I learned:

- **Pay attention to the little things.** The Temptations recognized that it wasn't good enough to just sound good; they wanted to give the audience the total experience. They had precision in every step and each hand gesture. Paying attention to the details will always set us apart from the competition.

- **Persistence is key.** We all know the expression "hang in there," but how many of us give up on our goals when the going gets tough? It is easy to get discouraged when things don't work out in our favor right away. One of the early Temptations group members gave up after a few songs didn't launch the group into immediate fame and fortune. There is no such thing as an overnight success. If we believe in our dreams, we have to be willing to keep working until our hard work pays off.

- **Don't be distracted by outside influences.** It is easy to get distracted by all the peripheral things that pop up on our radar screens. Whether it is negative people, activities that do not support our life purpose, or just plain time wasters (I'm still working on my Spider Solitaire addiction), we have to stay focused on the end result that we are committed to achieving. One group member allowed alcohol to destroy his focus and, ultimately, his gift.

- **Pride goes before a fall.** He had it all! Fame, fortune, and a following of energetic fans. Sometimes the accolades can go to a person's head, as it did with one of the group's members, to his ultimate detriment. We have to remember to stay grounded and understand that it is not about us. We are to use the gifts we've been blessed with, but understand that we were given those gifts to impact others, not just for self-glory.

- **Change is inevitable.** As with every area of life and business, musical styles are subject to change. Trends come and go. It would be difficult to think of a group that went through as many creative and personnel shifts as the Temptations. They understood that in order to remain successful and relevant, they had to change with the times. We have to recognize that economic and business fluctuations demand that we constantly sharpen our existing skills and develop new ones.

In school, we are given the opportunity to learn lessons before we have to apply them. Life isn't usually that way. The lessons are thrown at us, and we sometimes gain our knowledge from experience. In our relationships, finances, business, and health, we often attend the "school of hard knocks." I think a better way to learn is to apply the lessons you gain from others as you go through life. If I see that someone else's hand is burned, I'm willing to believe that the stove is hot! I'm planning to keep these lessons in mind as I press toward my goals, and I hope you will, too.

SPRING INTO YOUR GOALS

"In the spring I have counted 136 different kinds of weather in 24 hours."

MARK TWAIN

Wow—Mark Twain must have lived in Chicago! The weather has been up and down here, but I think it is official: at the time of this writing, spring has finally sprung, even in the Windy City! It takes a rough winter for us to really appreciate the spring. Similarly, it takes difficulty for us to truly appreciate growth and blessings. The good thing is that no winter lasts forever; it is always followed by spring. You've hung in there through the winter of life and now it's time for things to bloom. Seventeenth-century poet Anne Bradstreet wrote, "If we had no winter, the spring would not be so pleasant: if we did not sometimes taste of adversity, prosperity would not be so welcome."

If you are going through a "winter" season in your life, be encouraged that spring is just around the corner. Spring symbolizes rebirth; it instills a sense of hope and joy. The last bit of snow has melted and buds are finally beginning to show up on the trees. In anticipation, we wonder, "What's next? What's around the corner?" Whether it is business growth, a new job, an addition to the family, or a new relationship, we are always excited about the promise of things to come. Your personal spring is not dependent on any calendar. Your spring is whenever a new season is beginning in your life.

How do you get started on your goals when you're coming out of a winter season and entering another spring? There's a saying: "What's the best way to eat an elephant? One bite at a time." I hope that analogy made sense to you. I tried using it on my students recently and they looked at me blankly. One asked, "Why would you want to eat an elephant?" I felt old.

Often our goals seem too monumental for us to ever achieve. A goal that is overwhelming can actually be disempowering. By breaking your goals down into smaller tasks that you can complete each day, you can begin to chip away at the big goals until they are reduced to manageable "bites." I work with my clients to develop long-term goals, which we drill down into short-term goals, monthly objectives, and then daily action items. It is only at the task level that you really begin to make monumental progress. Just like the elephant is much too large to tackle in one sitting, major goals can seem insurmountable if viewed as one large project.

My business partner, Kiela Smith-Upton, and I created a system called Daily Disciplines to keep ourselves and our clients on track with our goals. I've found that the focus the system creates has allowed me to at least triple my productivity, which, in turn, raises my level of excitement through the roof! (Whoop, whoop!) I can get so much more done in a day when I plan it out in advance as individual tasks. And it gives me a greater sense of accomplishment just to get small tasks done. There's just something about scratching things off a list that makes me feel good. Sometimes I'll add something that I already did but forgot to write down, just so I can scratch it off. I don't consider it cheating.

If your goals seem like too much to handle, try breaking them down. Decide what you can do within the next month. Then break those monthly goals down into daily and weekly tasks that are achievable yet will stretch you beyond your current comfort zone. Remember to include a reward on your list of things to do as you pass even smaller milestones. Looking forward to a reward is motivating in itself.

Whatever you plant during a new season of your life will soon begin to bud and sprout. Just remember that it needs to be cultivated in order for it to bloom. It is never too late to cultivate your gifts. So, think about it: Is there a purpose in you that you are not releasing? What gifts and talents are you robbing the world of by holding them inside?

What better time than now to get moving on your goals and dreams. Start eating that elephant!

CREATE A VISION-DRIVEN LIFE

"We are limited, not by our abilities, but by our vision."

UNKNOWN

Okay, be honest. How many of you are still sticking to the resolutions you made for yourself at the beginning of the year? I used to make a very impressive list of New Year's resolutions. I gave that up several years ago. I was cleaning my office as I was writing my resolutions, and I came across my list from three years before. Guess what was on that list? You got it: the same things that were on the list I was creating at the time. At that point, I understood that simply making resolutions would not create any lasting change in my life. So, if you're still making New Year's resolutions, tear them up! It's time to create a larger, more focused reality for your life. It is time to bring your goals and visions into fulfillment and move forward in your dreams.

What specific visions do you have for your life? Are you truly living with purpose, passion, and faith? You can create the life you want for yourself if you understand your purpose, follow your passion, and have the courage to step out on faith. We are all born with gifts and talents that the world is waiting for. We have to be bold enough to bring our visions into reality no matter what obstacles we encounter.

Everything around you began with a vision. Everything was created first in someone's imagination before it became a reality. And it all was created from materials that already existed, whether it was the first airplane created by the Wright brothers or the chair you might be sitting on right now. Someone had a bold enough vision and believed in that vision strongly enough to make it reality. Walt Disney had a dream to build a theme park focused on a mouse! It is said that he was turned down by 301 banks before he got a loan to build Disneyland. Jack Canfield and Mark Victor Hansen were turned down by 144 publishers before one took on the first *Chicken Soup for the Soul* book, and it became a best-selling series worldwide! They say it took Thomas Edison 10,000 tries to make the incandescent light bulb. Can you imagine what his friends might have been saying? "You're going to make a *what*? A light bulb?" What do you think his wife was saying around experiment number 8,072? "Why don't you go out and get a real job?" What visions do you have for your career? Your personal life? They are no crazier than the examples you just heard. You can turn them into reality, as well. It might be difficult, but it's not impossible.

Each season of your life represents a fresh start—with new goals, new dreams, and a new outlook. If last year was good, this year can be even better! Wipe the slate clean. It is time for a new beginning! It is time to lose that extra 10 (or 30 or 50) pounds. It is time to refocus on your business plans and career goals. It is time to have meaningful relationships in your business and personal life.

Take the time to focus on *you*. Focus on what makes you feel happy and fulfilled. Understand your core values, and decide what you are and are not willing to compromise on. Have an honest conversation with yourself about who you really are, what you bring to the table, and what you want out of life.

I've found that one of the best ways to clarify your vision and accelerate your ability to create that vision is through the creation of a vision board. A vision board is a visual representation of all the goals and dreams you have for your life. I have two vision boards that I look at each morning—one for my business and one for my personal life. I've found that it helps in creating focus for the day.

,77777777777777xxxxxxxxxxxxxxxxxxxxxxxxxxxxxxxxxxxxxxxxxxxxxxxx777777777777xxxxxxxxxxxx777xxxxxxxxxxxxxx back, and make the changes you need to make in your life in order to attract what you seek.

Free yourself from guilt, bitterness, and regret. Carrying baggage into the future is like trying to drive a car by looking in the rearview mirror. Unpack those bags, and start again with a fresh outlook. Be grateful for your blessings. Appreciating what we already have is the cornerstone of life satisfaction. It only gets better from there!

With a positive outlook, the world can be your oyster. If you are not satisfied with your past, begin again. This is the time to do it. Pastor Jerald January said, "God blesses action, not ideas." It is time to get our goals and ideas out of our heads and into the universe. It is a new year, and it is time for action! Always be open to new possibilities. You never know what is just around the corner.

IT'S ALL ABOUT RELATIONSHIPS

"The most important ingredient we put into any relationship is not what we say or what we do, but what we are."

STEPHEN R. COVEY

I've written a lot about relationships over the years, but trust me when I say I'm no expert on the subject. However, I do know that when it comes to relationships, most often we tend to focus on what the other person is or is not. We focus on what we want to get out of the relationship. We also think about the types of people we want to avoid based on our past experiences. How often do we really take ownership for our own roles in the success or failure of our relationships? How often do we think about what we need to put into a relationship instead of what we want to get out of it? It is important to realize that we have to bring the things into our relationships that we expect of others. So, let's look at all the relationships in our lives and think of ways we can enhance those relationships by adjusting our own thinking and behavior.

There are certain principles that apply to all types of relationships, whether they are friendships, romances, business associations, or family interactions. We all lose focus from time to time and can benefit from being reminded of the core tenets of relationship success. Being attuned to them can help you make all your relationships healthier, happier, and more productive. I call these principles the Seven Be's:

Be Realistic

- **Know what you want.** Be honest with yourself about the types of relationships you want to have and the qualities and characteristics of the people you want to play major roles in your life. Know what you will and will not accept or settle for.

- **Know what is available.** Be realistic in your expectations of others. We all have faults. Understand that there are no perfect people, and don't expect to find perfection.

While it is easy to see the flaws of others, we have to keep in mind that they are dealing with ours at the same time.

- **Know where to find it.** Where you look for people to interact with determines the qualities you are likely to find in those people. Determine the types of people you are looking to attract into your life and frequent the places where those people are likely to appear.

Be Authentic

- **Know what you have to offer.** Be what you seek. If you are looking to interact with people who have certain qualities, be sure that you have developed those qualities in yourself. Do not expect more from others than you bring to the table yourself.

- **Know what others are looking for.** People often make the comment, "Take me as I am." It is important to keep in mind that just as you seek certain qualities in those with whom you interact, others have their own standards of what they are seeking. If you develop qualities that are attractive to others, you will have no problem drawing quality people into your life.

- **Know how to present your "best self."** To have the best, you must be your best. Be sure that the person others see reflects the best you have to offer.

Be Open

- **Know how to share.** Communication is vital to healthy relationships. Talk, listen, and ask questions. Sharing information is the best way to bond.

- **Know how much to share.** Be generous in sharing yourself, but do not overwhelm others with too much information too soon. Share relevant information as it is appropriate.

Be Tactful

- **Know when to share.** Handle your relationships with kid gloves, not a wooden mallet. Always be sensitive to how your words and actions will affect someone else.

- **Know what to share.** Some things are better left unsaid. The truth should always be couched in kindness. And make sure you have the facts correct.

Be Flexible

- **Know when to go with the flow.** Even good relationships require compromise. Sometimes it is good to "go along to get along." There does not have to be perfect agreement or conformity, but a healthy amount of compromise leaves everyone a winner.

- **Know how to extend yourself.** Sometimes it is necessary to go the extra mile for someone you care about. This might mean opening yourself up to their friends and family, doing a little something extra to make that person feel special, or just being a supportive shoulder or listening ear when they need it.

- **Know when to try something new.** Interacting with others can take us out of our comfort zones. Trying something that the other person enjoys might open you up to new and exciting experiences and could be a wonderful opportunity for personal growth as well as the growth of the relationship.

Be Accountable

- **Know how to be true to your word.** Always follow through on what you say you will do. If you find it impossible to keep a plan or promise, always let the other person know well in advance. This is the best way to build and maintain trust.

- **Know how to ensure your integrity.** Have an accountability partner, establish realistic deadlines, and determine nonnegotiable boundaries for the relationship.

Be Patient

- **Know when to wait.** Often we want to rush through things just to get to what we want. It is important to recognize when a potential relationship is worth the effort to take a step back and wait for things to develop at a pace that will be comfortable for both parties.

- **Know how to wait.** Waiting does not mean inactivity. Constantly work on self-improvement and stay engaged in worthwhile activities, while giving others the amount of space they need. Evaluate the feasibility of the relationship—while you are waiting, you can again consider whether the relationship meets your needs. This takes you back to the first point: be realistic.

Thus, we reveal a never-ending loop that keeps us evaluating and improving where we are in our relationships. The "buzz" is, by implementing these steps, you will build quality relationships. Here's to your relationship health!

FIGHT A BARREN LIFE

"Jesus never cursed a fig tree because it bore too much fruit and some spoiled. He only cursed it when it was barren and did not produce anything."

EDWIN LOUIS COLE

One day, I was out walking on the lakefront with a friend. We walked all the way to my favorite spot at the museum campus where there is a beautiful view of the Chicago skyline. On the way back, we saw a large tree that we'd noticed several weeks before. Although the tree was still standing tall and erect, it was completely barren. There were no leaves at all on the branches. That would not have looked strange in the winter, but during the middle of summer it looked odd among the other trees.

We had passed the tree on a previous walk, and my friend had commented that she thought the city should cut the tree down since it was obviously dead. This time, several weeks later, we noticed that there was a large orange *D* painted on the trunk of the tree. We surmised that the *D* stood for *demolition*. Apparently, we weren't the only ones who'd noticed the tree was barren. It might have taken some time for it to catch someone's attention, but the tree's lack of fruit had been detected.

It is the same way with our lives. We might be standing tall and erect just like the tree, but we could be dead on the inside. Sometimes we can pass it off by telling people that everything is fine—and, in certain seasons, we might be able to get away with it. We can dress up in the latest fashions, drive the finest cars, and have our hair perfectly coiffed while making a six-figure income. But it is only a matter of time before a barren life begins to show on the outside. In our quest to do and be and have, we might not even notice it ourselves for a while. We can fill our lives with many empty activities and many "things" that really have no long-lasting impact on our lives or anyone else's. This is where the barrenness comes in. After a while, we begin to wonder why we are no longer satisfied with our lives, although we have a good job or a nice home or a lovely family. We begin to feel that something is still missing.

People handle this feeling in different ways. Some people cheat on their spouses or date multiple partners to find that extra fulfillment that they believe they deserve. Others turn to comfort food (which will eventually make them very *uncomfortable* in their clothes). Some become thrill seekers, trying things like skydiving and free diving in the hopes that these extreme activities will fill the void. And some think that making more money will do the trick. But still the branches are barren. And as we raise the bar, we seek to do and have even more to find fulfillment.

In a society focused on getting instead of giving, how do we stop this cycle? What is it that truly gives us the buds, leaves, and flowers that are signs of a fruitful life? No matter how much money we have, what types of cars we drive, how important and influential our associates might be, it is only by truly giving of ourselves that we can eliminate the barrenness in our lives. I recently attended a birthday dinner for a woman I know. As friend after friend came to the microphone to pay tribute to this vibrant 60-year-old woman, the theme quickly became obvious. Throughout her lifetime, she has been loved by children and adults alike because of her loving, giving spirit. She doesn't set much store by material wealth, and she willingly gives to others, even people she doesn't know—people who end up becoming lifelong friends. She gives her time, her talents, and the joy in her heart—a joy that automatically transfers to others when they are around her.

Next time you're feeling barren and unfulfilled, focus on what you can give of yourself to others. Soon you'll notice the buds of fulfillment and the leaves of contentment starting to sprout in your life.

MORE IS NOT ALWAYS BETTER

"Never allow your day to become so cluttered that you neglect your most important goal—to do the best you can, enjoy this day, and rest satisfied with what you have accomplished."

OG MANDINO

I realized something about myself the other day: I'm a pack rat. Okay, I didn't just realize it; I've known it for years, but I am just admitting it to you. And I'm realizing more and more the impact that this has on my life and business. My productivity is much higher when my brain is less cluttered, and my brain is less cluttered when my environment is less cluttered.

If you are anything like me:

- No matter how many times you clean the papers off the coffee table, they somehow magically reappear during the night.

- No matter how many bags of clothes you give away to charity, the closets never get any emptier.

- Somehow there are files from 1997 in the file cabinets while the current files end up somewhere else.

Well, it's time to get organized! My business partner, visual artist Kiela, and I do vision board workshops. We talk about the power of the mind and how anything ever created in reality was first created in someone's mind. So, it would follow that if our minds are cluttered, we'll create clutter in our reality—in our work, our environment, our relationships, and any other life area. Each area impacts the other. We need to focus on creating clarity in every aspect of our lives.

I attended an event recently where the host gave away several door prizes. One of the prizes went to whoever had the oldest receipt. Well, believe it or not, a lady had a receipt in her purse from 1987! She won the prize, of course (I hope it was a gift card for an organizing system), but what useful purpose could that receipt possibly have served? We might laugh, but think about some of the things we allow ourselves to hold on to.

There is a saying that "whoever has the most stuff wins." Well, that isn't necessarily true. Some of us fill our time with so many activities that we don't have time to relax. We fill our bodies with so much food that we ruin our health. Or we fill our homes with so much clutter that we barely have room to move. Any time is a great time to get rid of some of the excess that we've been holding on to. Here are some basic tips that will get your home, office, and brain ready for maximum achievement in your personal or professional life:

- **Determine which areas of your home and/or office need care, and rank them according to priority.** If entertaining is your priority, maybe you want to start with the kitchen or living room. If business is your priority, maybe you want to start with the office.

- **Determine your goals for each area.** How do you want the area to look and feel when you're done? What do you want that area to be ready for? If you want more business, make room in your file cabinets for the new clients' folders. If you want a spouse, stop sleeping with your laptop; put it back in the office where it belongs. Make space for whatever you are expecting.

- **Rather than going at it randomly, attack one area at a time; that way you can make a noticeable difference.** It is easy to get distracted as we move from room to room, because we see something in each room that needs to be done. When we jump from room to room, we don't make a big enough impact in any one area. If we force ourselves to focus on one room at a time, we will see change right away that will lift our spirits and encourage us to continue working.

- **Set a time limit for each project.** Block enough time to make a real difference, but not so much that you burn yourself out. Take a break at designated times to relax and refresh yourself.

- **Touch each item only once.** Either follow up, file, donate, or discard as appropriate. Once this becomes a habit, it will save a lot of time in the long run and keep things much more organized. Once you've taken the major steps to organize your space, get into the habit of small daily tasks to keep it that way.

- **As you organize, create an environment that is positive and inviting for each space.** For example, I've found that I'm a lot more productive if I actually work in my office. For a long time I didn't do that, because my office just wasn't an appealing space. I corrected that by sprucing it up. I bought a desk organizer and some blingy new accessories. I added a vision board over my desk, which replaced a black-and-white print of field-workers from the Art Institute—not exactly inspirational. Now I can look at color pictures of what I want to see in my future to inspire me as I work.

- **Have some fun!** I'm a big advocate of fun. Play some music while you're organizing, buddy up with a friend to make it a challenge, or find some other way to make the process more enjoyable.

Some of the clutter we're holding on to might not be physical. Many things clutter up our lives and take the focus off what is really important. Think about your mind, your time, your health, your relationships—what is adding clutter to any facet of your life? If you have extra unhealthy stuff in any area, it impedes your progress in all areas. Clearing out space mentally and emotionally makes room for growth, productivity, and peace of mind. Here are some tips to keep other types of clutter under control:

- **Let go of anything that doesn't serve a positive purpose in your life.** This includes emotional "baggage" from your childhood or past relationships.

- **Clear your schedule of menial tasks so that you'll have time to do the things that are really important to you.** The clutter of unimportant tasks can inhibit you from being available when a meaningful challenge comes along.

- **Rid yourself of human clutter.** Are there people in your life who are wasting your time or depleting your energy? Are there people who are space fillers, time wasters, or emotional vampires? Reevaluate those relationships and decide which might need to go.

These are just a few ideas; I'm sure you can think of others. Remember that whatever you don't control, controls you. More is not necessarily better. Make a commitment to let it go!

JUST BE HONEST ABOUT IT

"To effectively communicate, we must realize that we are all different in the way we perceive the world and use this understanding as a guide to our communication with others."

TONY ROBBINS

Recently, a local Chicago high school's baseball team forfeited a game with a school on the other side of town. Here's what happened: Right before the game, the visiting team (from the North Side) issued a statement that said parents feared for their children's safety if they went to the field on the South Side. That statement was quickly recanted and the missed game was explained as being due to a problem with travel arrangements, a shortage of players on the visiting team, and so on.

I don't usually use my writing as a forum to rant, but something about that whole scenario bothered me. It wasn't so much that there was a general fear of the South Side. What bothered me more was that the visiting team decided to make up an excuse to save face. There seems to be a real fear of open communication in our society. No one wants to admit they just did or said something dumb. But we all do—trust me, I speak from experience. And, in any case, if an issue is to be resolved, it must be acknowledged and addressed with total honesty. Covering it up will only cause resentment and anger to fester. Think about it. Wouldn't it have been better for the North Side team to acknowledge their fears? Chicago has been in the news a lot regarding issues of violence, and it is a frightening thing. There is nothing wrong with parents being concerned about the safety of their children. But I don't believe that having the students at both schools meet downtown for a media-pacifying breakfast did much to address or alleviate those fears. Only honest conversation will give both sides a better understanding of each other and of the issue. Avoiding the truth never solves anything. Neither does sugarcoating it.

How about if—no, make that *when*—we say or do something dumb or something that offends another person, we just own up to our mistake and use it as an opportunity to build understanding and improve the relationship? The initial conversation is never easy because we don't know how the other party will react. None of us likes confrontation. But isn't it better to take a chance on making things better than to continue to pretend that everything is all right when it really isn't?

The good news is that when we reach out to others with a positive and open attitude, things usually do get better. If you have a difficult conversation looming in your future, here are a few tips to keep in mind:

- **Don't be afraid to admit you were wrong.** A heartfelt apology is not a sign of weakness; it is a sign of strength of character.

- **Try not to give with one hand and take with the other.** It is very easy to blame the other person while apologizing for our mistake. We might feel that we're being the bigger person by apologizing, but if that apology is lined with criticism, it only creates more negativity.

- **After you've said your piece, shut up and listen.** Give the other person time to react and to openly and honestly share his or her feelings. Keep in mind that while you've had time to think about what you were going

to say, the other person might not have.
Their initial reaction might not be exactly
what you were hoping for. Give them time
to absorb your comments and sort out their
own feelings before responding negatively
to anything they might say.

Above all, to loosely quote Saint Francis of Assisi, let's seek more to understand than to be understood. All our relationships would benefit from having a better understanding of the other perspective. Hopefully we can all learn from past mistakes and move forward with even stronger relationships. By the way, if you don't live in Chicago, the two schools rescheduled the game and all went well.

LESSON #31

FORGIVENESS HELPS US HEAL

"Resentment is like taking poison and waiting for the other person to die."

MALACHY MCCOURT

One day, I was visiting the father of a close friend who was in a nursing home. He was a very loving man who claimed all his daughter's friends as his own, since our fathers were no longer alive. We all called him Dad. Although he was the one whose health was fading, he never failed to speak words of encouragement to all who came to visit, as well as to the staff who worked in his ward. He was the most popular resident in the ward, and no one ever left his presence without feeling uplifted and encouraged.

On that particular visit, he wanted to talk to me about my writing. He shared his belief that writing was my gift

129

and that I needed to focus more on it. He gently scolded me for putting so many other things ahead of my writing. Although I'd never discussed the subject with him, he rightly concluded that I was trying to do too many things and not focusing on what God was really calling me to do. He spent much of our visit insisting to me that others will be impacted through my writing, not through many of the other pursuits that I tended to dabble in.

Suddenly, the conversation shifted, and he made a statement that seemed to come out of nowhere. He said, "You know you have to forgive. You're not hurting anyone but yourself if you hold a grudge against someone. They are going about their business and you are the only one who is mad." Then he went right back to talking about my writing.

I was stunned! How did he know? There was a person against whom I was definitely holding a grudge. I thought about it constantly, and fumed, but I had never discussed it with anyone. I know that no one could have told him. But somehow he knew what I needed to hear at that particular time. I never asked him how he knew (I think I figured that one out myself); I just nodded and said, "You're right, Dad."

I had been praying about forgiveness in that particular situation, but I didn't really have an attitude of forgiveness. I had more of an attitude of anger and retribution. I said that I wanted to forgive, but I really wanted revenge. As time went on, I continued to pray about it, and the hurt and anger began to subside. I won't say that it was an overnight occurrence—it was definitely a process—but I soon began to turn all that negative energy around.

The first step to emotional healing is forgiveness. If we harbor resentment from old wounds in our hearts, we are unable to move forward in our purpose because the bitterness we carry will drag us down. We often believe that the recipient of our ire will somehow fare badly because of whatever they did to anger us. In reality, that person has probably forgotten about the incident and those of us who are holding on to the anger suffer the most.

Negative emotions can be toxic if we allow ourselves to marinate in them. We might look just fine on the outside—like when you wash your car on the outside, but the backseat and the trunk are piled up with junk (not that I'd know anything about that firsthand). We are carrying around extra weight that is slowing us down mentally, physically, and emotionally. Heavy things constantly carried in the trunk will eventually wear down the shocks on your car. Anger and resentment carried around in our hearts will eventually wear us down, steal our joy, and possibly even ruin our health.

When we focus on the negativity of past hurts and "baggage," we allow others to control our emotions, and they don't even know it. As "Dad" said, they are going on with their lives and we are the ones who are hurt by our attitude.

If you are harboring unforgiveness toward someone, even if that someone is you (we are sometimes most unforgiving of ourselves), make a pledge to yourself that you will let it go. You'll be amazed at how much lighter your trunk will be.

DON'T BE AN ELEPHANT

"What the mind of man can conceive, he can achieve."

NAPOLEON HILL

Ever wondered how an elephant is trained? At an early age, they are tethered to a pole and allowed a small range of motion. They are trained to circle around within that range. When they try to move farther away than the chain allows, the chain is jerked and it hurts. As they grow older and bigger, they are easily able to break free of the chain, but they don't try because they remember the pain associated with stretching outside the boundaries. Because they are conditioned to stay within the range of their training, they never break free of their constraints.

It might look really odd when you go to the circus and you see those huge animals docilely walking around in a small circle. But think about it. As humans, we typically condition our minds to stay within certain parameters, as well. We engage in internal conversations with ourselves all the time. Unless we're trained to examine these conversations, many of us don't even realize we're having them! We tell ourselves that we can't do certain things because we are too much of one thing or not enough of something else. And, thus, we find ourselves, much like the elephants, chained to a life of mediocrity. Who wants that?

How many times have we hesitated to stretch ourselves because we hear the echo of someone in our past, or maybe even our own voice telling us we're not smart enough, we don't have enough money, we're too short, or whatever our own "story" might be. Often what the voices are saying has no basis in reality, but we believe it because it's what we have always heard. If we expect failure, we tend to get it. If we expect success, it works the same way.

It is so much easier for us to focus on the negatives. They (whoever "they" might be) say that it takes five positive statements to replace one negative statement. So, we must learn to flip those negative statements into positive "I can" and "I am" statements that we can practice until we are more comfortable believing the positive statements than we are accepting the negative ones.

Success is a way of thinking. Shifting our mind-sets will shift our energy, which will lead us to positive action. Try it now. Write down a negative statement that you've thought or heard about yourself. Then turn that statement into a positive one, written in the present tense. For example, "I'm too old to do that" can become "I am full of energy and have plenty of time to achieve any goal I want in life." "It was all my fault!" can become "Mistakes were made on all sides. I take ownership for my part. I've learned and grown from the experience, and I'm ready to move forward!"

If we practice stretching our minds beyond the constraints we've put on them, we'll soon find that we'll begin to stretch ourselves to achieve more than we ever thought possible. Watch out, ringmaster. We're about to break free!

LIFE IS OUR GREATEST PERFORMANCE

"I'm a perfectionist; it's part of who I am."

MICHAEL JACKSON

When I noticed that Michael Jackson's *This Is It* video had just been released and was available at a Redbox near me, I decided to rent the movie for pure entertainment. Michael definitely had his share of personal issues and suffered an untimely death. But he was nothing short of an amazing performer. I expected to enjoy watching him sing and dance in the video. However, I was surprised at the lessons that jumped out at me. I immediately grabbed a pen and began to write. I now truly understand why Michael Jackson was the King of Pop. He focused on giving his best to his fans at all times. His incredible work ethic made him unstoppable. Here are some of the lessons I learned from M.J.:

- **Lead by example.** Michael gave as much as he expected from others. He required a lot from his staff, but he put in more time, energy, and effort than anyone. Those on his team never minded when he asked them to do more. When we lead by example, others will follow.

- **Treat others with respect.** Even when giving negative feedback, he always spoke to others with kindness. Kindness breeds respect.

- **Pay attention to detail.** Throughout the movie, I was awed by the incredible sets and special effects. There was precision in every move made by Michael and all his dancers. He would stop to correct and improve things that were already great to make them *exceptional.* Why settle for good when excellence is within reach?

- **Know when to push the boundaries.** Michael truly gave it his all. He was innovative and creative and often pushed the limits. Yet, at times, he held back, saying, "I have to save my voice on this one." It is important to know when to give our full effort and when to hold something in reserve for the future.

- **Be customer focused.** Michael strove to exceed audience expectations. "We want to take them places they've never been before." And he did just that. We should always think of ways to raise the bar.

- **Dress for success.** At every rehearsal, he dressed as if he were onstage. He wore blazers, sparkly pants, and so on, as if every rehearsal were a performance. If we want to be successful, we should remember that we are always "onstage."

Michael said, "It all starts with us. Or else it will never be done." Isn't that the truth? Whatever it is that we are called to do—whatever gift we have to give to the world— if we don't do it, it will never be done. If we adopt the tenets that Michael's success was based on, we can become a force in our corner of the world, just as Michael was in his. When we look at the "man in the mirror," who do we see?

APPRECIATE WHAT YOU HAVE

*"We tend to forget that happiness doesn't come
as a result of getting something we don't have, but
rather of recognizing and appreciating what we do have."*

FREDERICK KOENIG

If you have a Target obsession like I do, you can imagine my shock at the checkout counter one day when I noticed that the woman behind me in line only had one item on the conveyer belt! I had to look back a couple of times just to be sure. Finally, I couldn't take it anymore. I turned to the woman and said, "I have to say that I've never seen anyone come into Target and leave with just the one item they came in to buy." She replied, "Don't be impressed; I was here yesterday." I felt much less animosity toward her at that point, as I can never seem to leave Target without spending at least $100, regardless of what I went in to buy. But, don't worry, my Target 12-step program is helping with that . . .

A recent conversation with an associate turned to the subject of overpurchasing. I was very impressed as she discussed her antihoarding philosophy. She makes it a habit of giving away clothes that she doesn't wear so that her closets are never cluttered, and she grocery shops once a week, only buying enough for that week. She was raised to believe in using what you have and not holding on to extra "stuff." That goes so much against what most Westerners believe. For some reason, we always believe that more is better—whether it is clothing, square footage of our homes, food, or other physical pleasures. We often don't take the time to appreciate what we have in our ongoing quest to get more.

Right now, I make less money than I made when I was in corporate America; however, I wouldn't trade the experiences that I am having now for the money I made then. I have so much appreciation for where I am right now. I enjoy teaching, training, and speaking engagements. I love having the flexibility of working at midnight and playing during the middle of the day if I choose. I've learned I can be happier with less, and I still have way more than I need.

It is so easy to make ourselves slaves to acquiring more "stuff." It is always good to take the time to appreciate the things we already have and to give to others out of our abundance, rather than acquiring more things that we really don't need. So, excuse me for now—I need to go clean out my closets (again).

Your Passion Can Become Your Livelihood

"Nothing great in the World has been accomplished without passion."

Georg Wilhelm Friedrich Hegel

What is it that you really love to do? What are you really good at? Most of us had an unmistakable skill and passion for something that was evident at a young age. But many of us never learned to tap into that passion. For me, it was always writing.

As I mentioned earlier, I went a different route in life, listening to well-meaning teachers and counselors who advised me based on my skills but not my passion. For many years, I was not living in my purpose. I was not doing what

I was passionate about. However, I have come to the realization that it is never too late to follow your passion. For example:

Maya Angelou published her first novel, *I Know Why the Caged Bird Sings,* at age 41.

Julia Child enrolled in her first cooking class at age 37 and published her first cookbook at 49.

Margaret Rudkin, in her 40s, started a baking company in her kitchen. That company eventually grew and is now known as Pepperidge Farm.

Bernie Marcus, at 49, got fired from Handy Dan, a small hardware chain in Newark, New Jersey. Instead of getting depressed, he and another fired employee started their own hardware store—it's called Home Depot.

Ray Kroc founded the McDonald's Corporation at the age of 53.

Colonel Harland Sanders was in his 60s when he launched his fried chicken business. He went to over 100 restaurants before he convinced one to use his special recipe for fried chicken to provide quick and affordable meals for families.

Moses was 80 years old when God called him from tending sheep in the wilderness to lead His people out of Egypt.

Grandma Moses, the artist who died at 101, did not pick up a paintbrush until she was in her 70s.

What are you passionate about? If you feel like you have not achieved the levels of success you desire in various areas of your life, remember that you have everything you need to live a life of purpose. You just need to tap into your passion. Start writing a new chapter in your life today. What are you waiting for?

ACHIEVE YOUR DREAMS

"If you can dream it, you can do it. Always remember this whole thing was started by a mouse."

WALT DISNEY

I was lying on my new hammock, typing my some-what monthly newsletter, "EmPOWERed to . . ." (Yes, I have a hammock on my back porch. Sometimes I like to pretend that I'm on vacation while I work—don't knock it.) Anyway, I was lying on the hammock, being grateful for the warm fall day we'd been blessed with in Chicago, and I thought about the hammock that I had just thrown away. Embarrassingly, the hammock I'd bought the year before broke while I was lying on it, which resulted in me landing on the ground. Not cute. Although I know I've put on a few pounds, it wasn't because of that. Foolishly, I'd left my portable hammock outside all year, in the rain, snow, cold, and heat, and it just wasn't built for that. Instead of taking proper care of it (bringing it inside and storing it in its case), I was lazy and left it where it was, letting whatever happened to it just happen. The ropes faded and shrunk, and the stand rusted because of the elements.

There's a popular expression that some people *dream* of great accomplishments, while others are awake to actually *do* them. Sometimes we take the lazy approach with our dreams. We want to relax and enjoy success, but we leave our goals lying around, unattended, and let whatever happens happen. If we don't nurture and care for our dreams, they'll break down and die, just like the hammock. So . . . are you taking proper care of your dreams or are you just leaving them where they lie? Are you nurturing them and protecting them from the elements that would do them harm—the self-doubt, the naysayers?

Do all your actions connect with your fundamental life purpose? Dream achievers consciously decide to make their goals a priority in their lives—they want to maximize their gifts and talents. This doesn't necessarily mean they start out knowing exactly how they will achieve every goal, just that they have made the first and most important step, which is the decision that their dreams are important.

Most of us have goals for our personal and/or professional lives. We want to advance in our careers, grow our businesses, maintain a healthy lifestyle, achieve financial independence, and have successful relationships. But how often do we sit down and map out a plan to ensure that those things occur? Many of us have a financial plan or a business plan, but how many of us have a life plan? John L. Beckley said, "Most people don't plan to fail, they fail to plan." Studies indicate that those who put their goals and dreams in writing achieve much greater success in the areas they focus on.

Are you a dream achiever? For many, just a small step in the right direction can make a big difference toward your future success.

Here are some tips to help you ignite your dreams and get moving in the right direction:

- **Determine the top three life areas you'd like to see improved.** They can be personal or business-related.

- **Evaluate your current level of satisfaction in those areas on a scale of one to ten.** Be honest about where you are right now.

- **Write down three to five realistic tasks for each area.** Focus on action items that will increase your satisfaction when completed.

- **Set specific dates for achievement of each goal.** Make the time frames short enough to create a sense of urgency, but be sure to give yourself enough time.

- **Post the tasks where you will see them morning and night.** In your bedroom or on the bathroom mirror are good suggestions.

- **Monitor your progress along the way.** Actually seeing yourself moving forward will encourage you to do more.

- **Reward yourself as you reach major milestones.** It is great to have something to look forward to, and the celebration will give you a much-needed break before starting again.

By developing a life plan, creating SMARTER (specific, measurable, achievable, realistic, time-bound, energizing, and rewarded) goals, and breaking those goals down into manageable tasks that you focus on every day, you will immediately begin to see yourself growing closer to the realization of your life dreams. Taking personal responsibility for your progress toward your goals will energize you and ensure that you are playing your A game. Here's to achieving all your dreams!

EMPTY YOUR CUP

*"We are cups, constantly and quietly being filled.
The trick is knowing how to tip ourselves over
and let the beautiful stuff out."*

RAY BRADBURY

There is a saying: "Empty the cup. Every time you empty it, it comes back twice as full." Thanksgiving is the traditional time for expressing gratitude and appreciation for our many blessings, but we should have the spirit of Thanksgiving every day. Real wealth begins with giving. When we give, we open ourselves up to receive even more. Sometimes when I'm coaching people, I get so caught up in their excitement over breakthroughs that I feel like I'm getting more out of the sessions than they are. I feel so blessed to be able to grow right along with them as I'm sharing tools and information.

When you share your gifts with others, you will get a feeling of personal prosperity that has nothing to do with money. Here are several ways you can make a difference by pouring into the lives of others:

- **Give your time.** Babysit for someone who can't afford to hire a sitter. Take food to someone who is sick. Visit a nursing home. Send a note to brighten someone's day. Volunteer at a local organization for whatever cause you support—women, children, the homeless, even your favorite animal shelter.

- **Give your talents.** What can you do that would make a difference in someone's life? Can you knit? Style hair? Sing? Do you like to clean and organize? (Then come to my house! Just kidding.) Extend yourself by using your gifts to help and cheer others.

- **Give your blood.** Every two seconds someone in America needs blood. Currently, only 3 out of 100 people give. Every pint of blood can save up to three lives. Contact the Red Cross for information.

- **Give to a good cause.** There are many charities that are doing great things to help those who are less fortunate. Donating items from your home will not only give you a warm feeling, it will help you to create more space in your home. Rather than reinventing the wheel, consider giving money or items from your home to an established charity. Here are some suggestions:

- Joyce Meyer's Hand of Hope ministry is providing shelter, clean water, schools, and more in countries all over the world, including India, Pakistan, Haiti, and Zimbabwe.

- To help halt the cholera outbreak in Haiti, the International Preparedness Network provides LifeStraws, which filter drinking water for flood victims for a $5 to $10 donation.

- Consider donating clothes, children's toys, kitchen tools, books, furniture, or appliances to your local Salvation Army, Unique Thrift Store, or Goodwill. Some facilities have programs to give gently used business clothing to women who are seeking employment.

- Your old cell phone might seem outdated to you, but it can help someone. Contact the Charitable Recycling Program for collection sites across the United States.

- Donate your old glasses to your local Lions Club.

- Contact a local shelter, food bank, church, or the Boy Scouts of America to inquire about their current needs.

- **Give a surprise.** Offer a parking space to another driver, pay the toll for the next driver coming through the toll booth, give your server a bigger tip, pay for a stranger's meal at a restaurant, send someone a gift card "just because," or pick up a homebound person for an outing.

- **Give your organs.** Leave a lasting legacy. Register with your state and sign the donor form on your driver's license. A friend of mine who passed away recently was an organ donor. His family was notified that his organs helped 50 people.

I'm sure you can think of many more ways to reach out to others that are not on this list. The important thing is to touch someone else's life in your own special way. As you enjoy your own blessings, remember to reach out to others and share from your bounty as only you can.

THERE IS A SEASON FOR BUILDING

"These unhappy times call for the building of plans . . . that build from the bottom up and not from the top down, that put their faith once more in the forgotten man at the bottom of the economic pyramid."

FRANKLIN DELANO ROOSEVELT

Does the quote above sound familiar? During the Great Depression, when Franklin Delano Roosevelt was president, he stressed the importance of the common person as the building block for the recovery of our great nation. As we find ourselves in the midst of a recession, we must remember that each of us can take a part in the rebuilding of our nation and in the building of our own

153

success. Our actions impact not only our own families and bank accounts, but the world around us.

There is a story about a man who was out walking one day. As he passed a construction site, he noticed two men methodically stacking bricks on top of each other. Observing the demeanor of the men, he noticed that one man was working angrily, with a scowl on his face, but the other was smiling and whistling all the while. He approached the two construction workers and asked the first man what he was doing. With a glare, the worker barked in a harsh, raspy voice, "I'm stacking bricks." Undeterred, the man moved on to greet the second worker and asked the same question, "What are you doing?" The worker paused and his eyes lit up. With a smile, he answered proudly, "I'm building a cathedral!"

There is a season for everything, and that includes your time to impact the world around you. What legacy do you plan to leave? What steps do you need to take to put your plan in place? Are you moving from day to day, or do you have a focused plan that will lead you toward the achievement of your goals? Are you just laying bricks, or are you building a cathedral?

Now is the time to build your network, your business, your brand, your product line, your wealth, your self-esteem, your winning team, your self-confidence, your reputation.

Focus on whatever it is that you desire to build, and go after it with all your might.

I live in the Midwest, and in the colder climates, April is the beginning of construction season. Between the months of April and October, the ground is warm enough to easily dig a deep foundation for a building. During the winter months, the ground is not suitable for digging and cement will not pour evenly. Just as those who build great developments know how to schedule their work, we have to schedule our work in order to complete our goals in their season.

The forecast here calls for possible snow tomorrow, but by Friday we are expecting 80-degree weather. Only in Chicago! I've learned to maximize each day, because we never know what the weather will be tomorrow. Just as the building season is limited, so is our season for building the foundations of our careers or businesses, our financial futures, our families, and so on. So, let's dig deep while the ground is ripe! The building season is upon us. What are you building?

CREATE YOUR OWN REALITY

*"If we don't change, we don't grow.
If we don't grow, we aren't really living."*

GAIL SHEEHY

March marks the beginning of spring, according to the calendar, anyway. We associate spring with planting, new growth, and unlimited possibilities. In the spring, just as we plant the seeds of the flowers or plants we wish to grow, we can plant the seeds of the goals we are committed to achieving, and we will soon begin to see the tiny shoots of our dreams begin to sprout.

Many of us are concerned about the current economy. With record job losses, home foreclosures, and falling stock prices, we are all learning to re-create our reality. We realize that we must plant new seeds in order to reap a harvest in the current conditions. That requires creativity, determination, and patience. Unfortunately, the stage called "growing pains" can be very real. As we move from one phase of our lives to another, whether it is a career, lifestyle, relationship, or whatever, there can often be insecurity, fear, and hurt during the transition period. Often we don't see the results of the seeds we have planted for a while as most new growth takes place under the soil, where it is dark, cold, and lonely. The fertilizer that has been dumped on us doesn't smell too good, either, but it helps us to grow. The experience of having a business fail, or being downsized, or losing a loved one through death or divorce is just the fertilizer that will make us stronger.

In the current economy, it might become necessary to plant more than one type of seed. Diversification is the key to financial growth, and we must also cultivate diverse skills in order to succeed in life. We can no longer rely on the paradigms of the past; we must create a new reality.

Growth takes place from the inside out. Although it might seem as if things are not moving in a positive direction, it is just that the roots are still underground. Perhaps you laid the groundwork for an idea that did not come to fruition, or perhaps you made a networking contact that did not turn into a business relationship. Perhaps a financial investment has not paid off. Sometimes the harvest might seem delayed, but the seed is still germinating below ground. The time you invested, the lessons you learned, and the hard work you put in have not been ignored by the Creator. In season, your plans will start to sprout and grow. There are a few rules that are universal to any situation:

- **You must plant a seed in order for something to grow.** No planting, no harvest.

- **You must plant in fertile soil.** Don't waste your time and ideas on people who do not embrace your vision or who are not truly in your corner.

- **You must till the land to prepare it for growth.** Stir things up. Think outside the box to make the extraordinary possible.

- **You must make sure the plant gets water and sunshine.** Have a strategy to keep your vision in motion. Don't let it die before it reaches maturity. Network with others who will help you to cultivate your dream.

- **You must exercise patience while waiting for the harvest to ripen.** Don't give up on your goals. If you believe in the vision you have for your future, stand firm and stay the course.

Your ideas will soon sprout forth into the sunlight, and the harvest will be worth the investment. The longer you wait to plant, the more you delay your harvest. So, start planting now. And don't forget to invite me to the harvest celebration!

LET GO OF
THE WHEEL

"As your faith is strengthened you will find that there is no longer the need to have a sense of control, that things will flow as they will, and that you will flow with them, to your great delight and benefit."

EMMANUEL TENEY

A friend shared a story with me about driving in a terrible snowstorm with her mother. The car started to slide. She held tightly to the steering wheel, trying to regain control, as the car began to spin in circles.

The harder she fought to get the car under control, the more it spun. After much struggle, she thought to herself, *I give up!* She threw up her hands in surrender. Her car stopped spinning and began to slide toward the concrete embankment. Amazingly, it stopped just inches from the wall. My friend wasn't thinking clearly in that situation, because experts tell us that if our car is out of control, we should immediately let go of the wheel.

Sometimes we try to control the situations in our lives, and it seems the more we fight to work things out, the more out of control things seem to get. We fight desperately to save our relationships, our children, our jobs. It is at those times that we need to throw up our hands and turn the situation over to a higher power. When we let go, we allow God to work in our situations. But as long as we keep fighting for the steering wheel, our lives will continue to spin.

We often maintain a façade of being in control even when we are not. In my friend's situation, the lack of control was obvious to her, her mother, and to everyone driving by. In reality, there are times when no one but us knows that our lives are in a tailspin. There are other times when everyone can see that we are spinning out of control, even if we don't admit it to them. Lastly, there are times when we even fool ourselves that everything is going just fine and that the path we are on is perfectly straight.

Is there an area of your life where you need to throw up your hands and relinquish control? Is it time to give up the driver's seat? It takes a lot of faith to step aside when you really want to force things to go your way. But, sometimes, if you want your passage to flow smoothly, you just have to let go of the wheel!

FIND YOUR BLISS

*"Follow your bliss and the universe will open
doors for you where there were only walls."*

JOSEPH CAMPBELL

There's a familiar saying that the only thing that is constant in life is change. It is inevitable that everyone, at some point, will experience changes that can have both physical and emotional impacts if not managed correctly. Internationally known consultant William Bridges teaches that change—the outer shift—often happens very quickly. However, transition is an internal process that finds you somewhere along the spectrum of denial, resistance, exploration, and commitment. The old reality no longer exists, but the new reality has yet to be embraced.

Because I made a major career transition after many years in corporate America, it is very rewarding for me to work with people who are moving to a different place in some area of their lives. Building a career, a relationship, or a life plan is similar to building a house. Even when you've designed your dream home, periodic updates are needed to keep the look current and to keep things in good repair. What got you where you are right now won't necessarily get you to the next level.

So, during times of change, how do you create a new reality for your life—one that engages your bliss? At some point during your transition, you will need to evaluate your options, set clear goals, and take strategic, meaningful actions that will move you to the next level.

Evaluate Your Options

Whether a transition is voluntary or mandatory, many people are facing weighty decisions when it comes to their futures in the areas of careers, relationships, and health. Because of limited opportunities, these decisions might include the possibility of switching to a completely different industry, accepting an opportunity that has lower compensation, or even starting their own businesses.

So, how do you determine how your current skills will translate to another type of opportunity? Understanding the ingredients you're working with—your unique wiring and purpose—is critical to navigating change. As Stephen Covey said, "The key to the ability to change is a changeless sense

of who you are, what you are about, and what you value."
One way to really understand who you are and how you're
wired is to utilize a highly accurate, whole-person assessment
tool to help you identify and evaluate your gifts, interests,
personality, and thinking style. Assessing how these elements
intersect will give you a clear picture of whether you want to
continue on your current path or investigate other options.

What ultimately gives you fulfillment might not be
the obvious path. Analyze your situation and think carefully about all your options before making a decision.
However, don't let an overreliance on logic inhibit your
decision making. Listen to your inner voice and see what
your intuition is telling you, as well.

Set Clear Goals

Once your decision is clear, the real work can begin.
It is time to crystallize your goals and develop an action
plan. Utilizing a coach is one of the most effective ways
of creating focus during a transition. Get a coach—even
if you're at the top of your game. Every top athlete and
entertainer has someone who helps them to solidify their
goals and who pushes them to the next level both physically and mentally. You can't see the picture when you're
in the frame. We all need someone to help us gain clarity

and hold our feet to the fire. Whether your goals are career related or personal, accountability is essential.

Act Strategically

Employees are hired for their aptitude and skills; however, continuous success is determined more by attitude and habits. Many people are unsuccessful because they lack clarity on which behaviors and beliefs to let go of and which new ones to pick up.

Strategy is all about focus. In order to act effectively, decide what you really want. Abandon the idea of "doing it all" and focus your actions on the 80/20 rule. Get rid of the 80 percent that is not serving you. When we create too many goals, we lose focus on what is really important. Trying to play more than one sport didn't even work for Michael Jordan!

Once you have reassessed your skills and aptitudes, determined your options, and set your goals, your behaviors should be congruent with your desired outcomes. Those outcomes should be inextricably tied to who you are at your inner core. Thus you create a winning formula that allows you to live your bliss.

Choosing to live in bliss, in a way that is congruent with who you really are, is a radical act that sometimes requires difficult choices. It requires that you honor your personal values and dreams while creating focused goals and taking the actions that will create what you really want in your future. Change is not a threat, but an opportunity to embrace a new and, most often, improved reality.

LESSON #42

RELEASE THE PAST AND MOVE INTO YOUR FUTURE

"People have a hard time letting go of their suffering. Out of a fear of the unknown, they prefer suffering that is familiar."

THICH NHAT HANH

Have you ever tried to hold on to a season of life that was no longer where you belonged? Guilty as charged (I'm raising my hand). Maybe it was a job that was no longer a fit, but you were afraid to step out and try something new. Maybe it was a relationship that was negative or draining that you hesitated to leave because it was fa-miliar. Sometimes we want things from the past so badly, not because we think they are what is best for us, but just because they're what we're used to. There is a saying that "the devil you know is better than the devil you don't know." Many times we might be tempted to feel that way.

You might remember the story of the ancient Israel-ites who journeyed in the wilderness for 40 years when it really shouldn't have taken them more than 11 days or so to reach Canaan. What were the reasons for the delay of their promise?

- **Fear of "giants."** The Israelites were intimidated by their enemies. They were afraid to claim what had already been promised to them because they did not believe that they measured up to the competition. Sometimes we allow fear to hold us back from our dreams. We believe we don't have what it takes to succeed. We look at the accomplishments of others and don't believe we can achieve those or greater things ourselves.

- **Refusal to let go of the past.** The people kept looking back at the way things were. They were going through a tough time,

but instead of focusing on the future,
they looked back, longingly, at the past.
Although it was very uncomfortable at
the time, in retrospect, their time in Egypt
became a "comfort zone." They began to
glamorize it as a time of plenty—a roof over
their heads and a chicken (or goat) in every
pot. Sometimes we put on rose-colored
glasses when we look back on the way
things used to be instead of being honest
with ourselves about how it really was and
moving toward a brighter future.

- **Disobedience.** They just didn't want to
  follow the plan that had been laid out for
  them. They were determined to keep doing
  the things they were used to doing in their
  old lives. Sometimes repetitive old habits
  stop us from making progress in our future.

Because of their fear, disobedience, and refusal to let go of the things of the past, what should have been a short journey turned into a 40-year odyssey. Instead of focusing on where they were going, they continued to fret about where they'd been. They distracted themselves from their goals by re-creating the same behaviors that bound them over and over and kept them traveling the same route. (Doesn't this bush look familiar?) They walked around Mount Horeb countless times in their journey from Egypt to the Promised Land.

At times it seems as if we've been waiting a lifetime for the things we want to materialize. We look at mistakes we've made in the past, decisions that didn't turn out well, hurts that were inflicted on us, opportunities we missed, and so on. And we find ourselves walking around the same mountain over and over again, looking at the same bushes, rather than moving forward into our own Promised Land. At those times, we need to refocus on our goals, look at where it is that we are trying to go, and determine the best route to get us there. We might have to cut away some of the shrubs and thorns (know any people like this?) that might inhibit our progress.

Just as the Israelites complained about the length and difficulty of the journey, sometimes the journey from our wilderness to our Promised Land is tedious and long. We might be tempted, as the Israelites were, to murmur and complain and long for the familiarity of things in our past—relationships, jobs, friends. But, even though it can be uncomfortable and, at times, frightening, the journey always ends with us in a better place. We might think we see "giants" in our paths, in terms of some of the obstacles that stand in the way of our future success. If we allow those giants to intimidate us, we might convince ourselves that we can't achieve the success that is ours to claim. Once I was sad over the loss of a relationship and, as I dealt with the feelings of loneliness and hurt, I also had to acknowledge that that particular relationship was not even satisfying to me while I was in it. So why was I feeling sad that it was over? Because I was in a "wilderness period"—a period of wandering and not knowing exactly where I'd end up. The more I thought about it, the more I realized that I was just biding time in a relationship that was not fulfilling to me at all. Often change is difficult, and an uncertain future, while exciting at times, can be scary. We have to learn to let go of the familiar and have faith that our futures have already been ordained.

The good thing is that there is something to be learned from every experience. Even if it is not a good experience, there can be a lesson that will move you farther along in your purpose. Even when you get lost and even when it takes a bit longer than expected to arrive at your goal, you can get back on track as long as you keep moving forward.

JUST BE YOU

"Today you are you! That is truer than true!
There is no one alive who is you-er than you!"

DR. SEUSS

Someone once posed a series of questions to me: Are you who you really are? Or are you who you have become due to circumstances? If you take away your fears, your baggage, your pain, who would you really be? Are you really who you are? Or are you the person you've become? Who is the "you" that is underneath it all?

On the surface, all of those questions sounded a bit crazy to me at the time. However, the more I thought about it, the more I realized that our life experiences do shape us into becoming who we are. Positive experiences can have one effect on our character, and negative experiences can have another effect. It is up to us to decide what that effect will be.

For example, if an 18-year-old receives a large inheritance, he or she might or might not be mature enough to handle it. One might look on it as a blessing that he or she was fortunate to receive, and handle it with care and appreciation. Another could view it as an entitlement, get arrogant, and squander it away. In both cases, it was a good thing, but it was handled differently.

Likewise, a tragedy such as the murder of a loved one can cause one person to carry anger and hatred throughout their life, whereas another person might reach out to comfort those who are in a similar situation and, in some cases, to comfort the very person who murdered their loved one. Of these two people, who do you think will lead a happier and more fulfilled life—the one who held on to the anger or the one who released it?

If you take a small, scratchy pebble and hold it under your tongue, it will become more and more irritating over time, and it will eventually cause you a lot of pain and frustration. You will most likely end up removing it unchanged. But if you insert that same scratchy pebble into the mouth of an oyster, the oyster will coat the pebble until it becomes a pearl. The situation is the same; it is all in how the irritant is handled.

Only you can determine how your experiences will shape your future. Who do you ultimately want to be? How do you get to the core of who you really are? Often people live in the space of who they've become without really understanding who they really are. The most effective mirror is the one you hold on yourself.

HARD WORK MAKES IT EASY

*"If God sends us on strong paths,
we are provided strong shoes."*

CORRIE TEN BOOM

Anything worth having is worth working for. Whether it is a career, a relationship, or a lifestyle goal, we will only get results based on the amount of energy that we put in. We should not expect to get positive results in any area of our lives if we know that we didn't put any effort into that particular area.

I was dining at a Chinese restaurant awhile back, and, at the end of the meal, I received the requisite fortune cookie. I've never cared for the taste of the cookies (mainly because they're not dipped in dark chocolate), but I've always enjoyed reading the fortunes. I'd met with my mentor earlier in the day and I'd shared a business idea that I was working on. Therefore, I found it relevant that my fortune cookie that evening told me that "endurance and persistence will be rewarded." I do believe that hard work pays off in the end. Of course, my date's fortune cookie told him that the love of his life would appear in front of him unexpectedly (should I be insulted?). Failing to wrestle that fortune from his clutches, I decided that mine was still a good one.

Many people become frustrated when they don't receive the success they desire in some aspect of their lives. However, sometimes it is just a matter of hanging in there until the change they are waiting for arrives. Success is so much more appreciated when we actually have to put in some effort to achieve it. I used to play the piano, and I remember a particular piece that my piano teacher, Professor Jackson, had me learn. Right after the annual recital, I had to start learning the four-page classical piece for the next year. It seemed early to start practicing. After all, a year is a long time. Then I looked at the sheet music. Each page was increasingly difficult. It took me the entire year to be able to play the piece flawlessly from memory. I still remember the feeling of accomplishment when I finally had it perfected. I wouldn't have had that feeling if I'd just sat down at the piano and played it flawlessly the first time he handed me the music. It was the result of my 365 days of hard work (okay, I didn't practice every day, but you get the point) that gave me the feeling of satisfaction in my achievement. That is also what made my playing seem effortless even while I was petrified at playing in front of an auditorium full of people—and being last on the program, no less!

Endurance and hard work definitely pay off. And when people see the result of your toil and dedication, they'll say, "Wow, you sure make that look easy!" Don't worry; it will be our little secret . . .

HARNESS THE POWER OF NO

"People think focus means saying yes to the thing you've got to focus on. But that's not what it means at all. It means saying no to the hundred other good ideas that there are."

STEVE JOBS

Is your plate piled high with endless tasks and deadlines? Are those around you—boss, parent, spouse, children, friends—making demands on your time based on their expectations of you? I am a person of varied interests. I like to learn and experience new things and meet new people. That presents a challenge to me as I focus on growing my business. I meet so many interesting people who are doing such interesting things. And they often want me to join them in whatever they are doing.

But I have ideas and goals of my own that deserve my focus more than the ideas and goals of others.

I have, at times, allowed others to hijack my schedule. Once it was a potential business partner who had some great ideas but wanted everything done his way, on his schedule. I have allowed it at other times with networking associates who had their own business goals. In many cases, after spending the time on their agendas, I reviewed my list of open items and regretted the time that I'd given away.

There is definitely nothing wrong with going the extra mile at times to help others. In fact, I strongly encourage stepping outside yourself to make a difference. However, if we say yes just to please others, without considering the cost, we are actually saying no to our own goals and dreams, which can cost us greatly in the long run. Not wanting to disappoint others when our schedules are already full can cause us to put our own goals on the back burner.

No is such a simple word, just two letters, one syllable. It kind of rolls right off the tongue. If you doubt that, just ask any two-year-old. We are all born with the instinct to preserve what is dear to us. But somehow, over the years, people manage to convince us it is rude to say no, even when the price of saying yes is too high. We often allow guilt to make us say yes to things that do not fit our goals, our values, our self-care, or our schedules. Saying yes might be easier, but it can cost us in time, stress, and lost opportunity at a later time.

Learn to say no to things that don't serve you. Your own priorities should be nonnegotiable. In order to achieve our goals, we have to maintain control of our schedules and not feel bad telling others that we are not able to meet their expectations at this time (or, sometimes, at any time). Overcommitting increases your stress level, which will impact your mood and your health. Be polite but firm. It is not always necessary to justify yourself, unless there is a boss–employee or spousal relationship.

Know your limits. If you try to be everything to everyone, you will end up doing too much. Others will take you for granted if you give yourself away. Just because you've always planned the department holiday party doesn't mean that you should continue to do it every year. Your situation might have changed, and your schedule might not allow your continued involvement.

Stick to your plan. Don't let others cause you to neglect your own goals. *Focus.* As much as we'd like to, we can't do everything, at least not well. (Remember what I said about multitasking?) Saying no to some things allows you to devote more time to the things you've already committed to do.

And be sure to get an understanding of exactly what is being asked of you before you commit to anything new, so that you will know how much time and effort on your part would be required. It's easy to want to impress others (especially at work) and seem like a real go-getter, but make sure you have the reserves to fulfill what's been asked of you. There may be someone else who can take it on. And, ultimately, it may not be worth your time and energy.

How do you determine which activities deserve your time and attention? Your work time should be focused on activities that engage and challenge you while supporting your business or career values and goals. Your personal time should be spent on activities that support your personal goals, including family, friends, health, relaxation, and so on.

When in doubt, it's okay to say, "Let me think about it." This will prevent you from creating false expectations and buy you some time as you review the proposal. Feel free to put limits on your involvement. For example, tell the person who is making a request that you will give them a set amount of time or that you will assist them on a day that better fits your schedule. Provide suggestions and alternatives: "I can't help you right now, but I can put you in touch with someone who might be better qualified to help."

I'm practicing my no even as I get interrupted while working on this chapter. It does feel empowering. In fact, I have even said no to myself, by skipping some of my newsletters, because it would interrupt my vacation goal (and that is a very important goal for me) and my other business goals.

Say it in plain English—no, nope, nah, uh-uh. Or try it in other languages—*nein, nej, non, nee, nai, nahin, nu, nae, hi, neni, nage, yuk.* Saying no can be both liberating and fun!

BOUNCE BACK

"No matter how far life pushes you down, no matter how much you hurt, you can always bounce back."

SHERYL SWOOPES, WNBA PLAYER, OLYMPIC ATHLETE

"A tree fell on my evergreens," my brother explained as the house tour led us to the wall of windows in the kitchen that looked out at his expansive backyard. "I hope they spring back." It was a concern that was voiced more than once over the next few days. Understandably, he wanted everything to be perfect for Mom's and my first visit, but who would have ever thought to hear such a statement from a conventional, somewhat chauvinistic male born and raised in Chicago? He'd only lived in rural Georgia for three and a half months. Was this the macho guy I grew up with? When did he ever notice a tree, let alone concern himself with its well-being?

On the last day of my visit (my mom was staying longer), I stood looking out the back window in my room at the grove of trees that lined the edge of the property, feeling somewhat sorry to leave. The woods beyond were full of barren trees—only a few red-and-gold leaves were left after being whipped by the wind. The grass was turning brown, and just a few flowers were still hanging on to their fading petals. However, as the other trees dropped their leaves to the ground, the evergreens were as full of vitality as always.

I noticed the two trees near the middle that had apparently suffered the brunt of the damage. They did look battered, I had to admit. Like my brother, I wondered if they ever would spring back. The good thing is that they were only bent, not broken. Thus, there was the possibility that the injured trees could eventually grow upright again. Perhaps the rain and the nutrients in the soil would strengthen their tattered limbs.

Often circumstances in our lives cause damage to our physical bodies or our spirits. We feel beaten down and whipped by life's challenges. But if we strengthen ourselves with the proper nutrients—physically, mentally, emotionally, and spiritually—we can recover and regain not only our original strength. We'll grow even stronger because of the experience.

By my next visit to my brother's house, those damaged trees had begun to grow back strong and straight. Soon you didn't even notice the difference between them and the rest of the grove. Similarly, when we bounce back from our troubles, we'll radiate with a vitality that will cause others to think that our lives have always been a bed of roses. We won't show outward signs of damage or trauma, but we'll know that the trials made us stronger and better for having endured them.

SOMETIMES ALL IT TAKES IS A HUG

*"It's easy to make a buck.
It's a lot tougher to make a difference."*

TOM BROKAW

A friend and her husband recently took on a beautiful labor of love. Her sister died and she and her husband decided to adopt her sister's two beautiful children, Charla-Jae (C.J.) and Judah, who at the time were about six and four, respectively, in addition to raising their own infant son. Children are so resilient. The two of them have the most beautiful eyes and the most beautiful spirits. Whenever I say hello or good-bye to C.J. and Judah, I always give them hugs. For a while, I felt a bit silly, because

I thought they might be thinking, *Who is this lady who is always hugging us?* Once we were at an event, and I'd given them my usual hello hug. As I was leaving, I decided not to bother them because they were sitting at a table eating cake. I made my way to the door. As I was standing at the door talking to someone, something made me look down. There was little Judah, standing beside me, looking up at me with the most beautiful smile. "Bye," he said, waving. "Bye, Judah," I replied, smiling back at him. He continued to smile and waved again. "Bye," he repeated. At that point, I realized that he'd come to find me because I hadn't given him his usual good-bye hug. I recognized at that point that you can never underestimate the little things. My hugs are nothing compared to the commitment of raising the children that my friend and her husband made. But any act of kindness that we show is generally appreciated by others.

In some of the vignettes in this book, we've discussed several empowerment principles—how to have success in our personal and professional lives by growing and building our businesses, careers, and relationships. There is much that we can do to empower ourselves to live in our purpose and to create the lives we imagine. Because we live in a nation ripe with opportunities and on the cutting edge of technological advancements, we tend to take for granted many things we should be grateful for. The opportunity to attend school, to practice the religion of our choosing, even to drink clean water from indoor plumbing—all are luxuries that much of the world does not enjoy.

We are all aware that we are in an economic recession. However, even in the midst of these troubling times, America is still a blessed nation, and we must be mindful of those who are less fortunate than us. Fifty percent of the world's population lives on less than $2 a day. Even during our worst times, we are better off than most.

We often get so busy running on the endless treadmill of trying to keep up, not only with our own expectations of ourselves but with others' expectations of us, that we can get into the mind-set that life is all about us—our new house, our new car, our new clothes. While it is great to strive to better ourselves in life, we must remember that only what we do for others will make a lasting impact on the world.

I read that Oprah Winfrey said, "Material success is rewarding and a lot of fun, but it's not the most important thing in my life because I know when this is all over, the Master isn't going to ask me how many things I owned or how many television shows I did. I think the questions will be: What did I do to make a difference? Did I learn to live with love in my heart?"

Whether it is starving children in a third world country, homelessness right in our own nation, or global warming—

we have to care about *something* outside ourselves, no matter large or small. We won't be remembered by the car dealer who sold us our Lexus, but we will be remembered by the student we mentored. We will not be remembered for the beautiful house we built for ourselves, but we will be remembered for the school we helped to build in a country without resources. What are you doing to leave a lasting impact on the world? What are you doing to make a difference? Sometimes all it takes is a hug.

WRITE A PRESCRIPTION FOR HEALTHY RELATIONSHIPS

"The purpose of a relationship is not to have another who might complete you, but to have another with whom you might share your completeness."

NEALE DONALD WALSCH

On the day after my birthday, I couldn't wait to run out and buy a stand for my new flat-screen TV. I got the stand on clearance because it was a floor model and had a few barely noticeable nicks—I do love a bargain! After I paid for it, the salesman had it wrapped, loaded onto a cart, and wheeled to the door. He casually asked, "What kind of car do you have?" "A Maxima," I told him. He looked a bit skeptical. "Are you sure it will fit?" he asked. "Oh, sure, we'll put it on the backseat," I replied.

Well, I'm sure you can see where this is going. The stand didn't fit, and I had to get a friend to bring it home a few days later in his truck. Everyone who saw the stand said the same thing, "What made you think that would fit in your car?" I guess I convinced myself that it would fit because I really wanted to take it home that day. I ignored the actual dimensions of the stand and saw what I wanted to see. I convinced myself that it would work despite evidence to the contrary.

We sometimes do the same things with the relationships in our lives; we want to make them "fit" for any number of reasons, but we need to take a hard look at the facts and be honest with ourselves. A few nicks are one thing, but how do we make a relationship work when the flaws are more serious?

Human beings have an inherent need to develop meaningful relationships. We all want to share our goals, ideas, joys, sorrows, desires, affections, and experiences with someone else. However, we all fall short at times in handling the mechanics of them. There are times when what we really need to do is "doctor" up or even perform "surgery" on some of our relationships. After all, we go to the doctor for regular checkups; why shouldn't we check on the health of our relationships? Just like your physical health, positive relationships—whether they are romantic, social, or professional—require maintenance. Good relationships don't just happen. Just as our physical bodies get sick from time to time, most relationships go through periods of illness, as well. Being constantly on guard for symptoms of illness within your relationships will help keep them healthy and prosperous. People who have healthy relationships are happier and less stressed.

Do you experience any of the following symptoms in any of your relationships?

- Frequent arguments
- Low-energy conversations
- Apathy or indifference regarding the relationship
- Lack of interaction and/or no desire for proximity
- Continuously looking for something better

If you answered yes to any of the above symptoms, you might be in an unhealthy relationship. If so, here are some possible remedies:

- **Get regular checkups.** To determine the overall health of your relationship, it is important to regularly communicate with your partner, friend, relative, or associate to determine how he or she is feeling about the rapport. Set a regular period, depending on the association (monthly, quarterly, etc.), to get together for the sole purpose of assessing the relationship.

- **Have a relationship checklist/chart.** Discuss what is working and what is not working in your relationship. Work on the issues and revisit them at the next check-in to see if the "stats" have improved.

- **"Weigh in" on your relationship.** Each of you should share your feelings with the other person. Be open and honest about what you are experiencing and listen carefully to his or her concerns.

- **Take the "temperature" of your relationship.** Is it running hot or cold? Do you still enjoy each other's company and/or benefit from the association? Is it moving in a positive direction?

- **Measure its "pulse."** Is it strong or weak? Is the bond between you growing stronger or weaker from one check-in to the next?

- **Use the correct prescription.** Know the right dosage of love and caring to share with that person, remembering that the prescription will be unique for each individual.

- **Know yourself.** Just as you pay attention to your body's signals when it is experiencing injury or illness, know your personal reactions to the situations you encounter in your relationship and how those situations affect you. Know your critical signs and how to interpret your results.

- **Read the warning signs/symptoms.** As indicated above, watch for key indications that there is a malignancy in your relationship.

Here are some of the vital signs of a healthy relationship and of the people in one:

- Is built on respect, trust, and caring

- Allows each person to be an individual and to grow personally

- Allows for differences of opinion and interests
- Apologizes, talks things out, and moves on
- Knows how to respect each other's "space"
- Enjoys each other's company
- Benefits from each other's opinions
- Supports each other's goals
- Contains open communication and sharing of thoughts and ideas, as well as active listening
- Establishes boundaries that the other knows not to cross
- Has common interests but also values differences
- Picks battles by determining what is really important and what issues are not worth arguing about and works on one issue at a time
- Says no when necessary
- Express appreciation for each other, to reaffirm respect and affection

In a healthy relationship, you should not be afraid to speak your mind. No type of relationship should cause you to compromise or doubt who you are. People who have your best interests at heart will never ask you to be someone you are not or to compromise what you believe in. Before being open with anyone else, you must first be honest with yourself about who you are, what you are seeking from another person, and what you are willing to give.

Remember, healthy relationships are not built overnight. It takes time, energy, and commitment to develop any type of relationship, whether with business associates, family, friends, or a romantic partner. Sometimes you'll find that no matter what you do a relationship just doesn't fit. If that is the case, don't force it. Sometimes it's better to relax and let it go.

LIFE IS NOT A BEAUTY CONTEST

"Happiness is beauty. Beauty is happiness. That is the true meaning of 'inner beauty.' . . . Shut out all commercials that seek to sell 'a better you.' There is no better you that can be sold to you by someone else."

ALICE WALKER

Liposuction, Botox, breast augmentation, laser hair removal, teeth whitening . . . It is estimated that approximately $14 billion was spent last year on cosmetic procedures. That doesn't even include the billions spent on fashion. (I, personally, adore the five-inch heels that hurt my feet after two hours.) Our culture puts a lot of emphasis on outward appearance and often determines one's worth based on physical form. The average woman feels inadequate if she doesn't look like the airbrushed models seen in magazines. But what really makes a person beautiful is what's on the inside. In the words of Marianne Williamson, "There is nothing Madison Avenue can give us that will make us more beautiful women. We are beautiful because God created us that way." True beauty comes from within.

How do others see beauty in us? It isn't the fashionable clothes we wear, the elaborate hairstyles, or the "bling." It's about having a beautiful temperament. Our beauty is demonstrated by our behavior. Do we show gentleness and quietness of spirit? Do we project peace and tranquility? Do we demonstrate love and harmony in our dealings with others, or do we easily take offense? If we believe that we need to give others a piece of our mind whenever we get angry, they will not see the beauty in us, regardless of how well we are dressed on the outside. Our inner being is much more valuable than what we look like on the exterior. I once worked at a job where there were a couple of women who wore scarves and pins emblazoned with spiritual words, such as *peace, love,* and *faith.* Unfortunately, those same women were the biggest drama creators in the department! The power of living a life of beauty is much more impactful than what we project on the outside. People will respond to the beauty inside of us, not what is *on* us.

We shouldn't depend on our outer appearance to make us beautiful. "Charm is deceptive, and beauty is fleeting" was stated profoundly in Proverbs 31:30. Physical beauty is momentary. No matter what we use to try to hold on to what we had, eventually it is going to go. And we'd better have something else there to replace it. Actress Halle Berry is quoted as saying, "Beauty? Let me tell you something—being thought of as a 'beautiful woman' has spared me nothing in life. No heartache, no trouble . . . Beauty is essentially meaningless, and it is always transitory." Lasting beauty only comes from inside and causes a person to be just as graceful and beautiful at 60 as at 20.

Let me be clear here: there is *nothing* wrong with getting your hair done, indulging in a mani-pedi, or wearing nice clothes. How you look does impact how you feel, and treating yourself well can boost confidence and self-love. Just remember that those things are temporary—you'll have to go back to the hair or nail salon for another visit, and you'll have to replace your clothes. Charm and beauty don't last, but inner beauty never fades. What's inside of us will always radiate outward to others.

BUILD YOUR TEAM

"The main ingredient of stardom is the rest of the team."
JOHN WOODEN

You've set your goals, but somehow you keep getting stalled on the road to achieving them. You are ready to run the next major play in the game of life. Who do you need to have on your team?

Someone might have suggested to you, "Get a coach!" That is excellent advice. There is immeasurable value in working with a professional sports or life coach, depending on your goals. A recent *Forbes* article reported that an overwhelming majority of people (83 percent) who have experienced professional coaching are satisfied with their experiences and would recommend coaching to others, according to a new study by the International Coach Federation. Whether used for personal fulfillment or professional goal achievement, coaching has been found to yield a return ranging from three to seven times its initial investment. Coaches help you create focus and clarity and provide the tools, structure, and ongoing support that will empower you to achieve your "stretch" goals. I have had a few coaches, and their help has proven to be invaluable. Through my first coach, Gerry, I learned lessons about accountability and stretching myself that I will never forget. My second coach, Donna, impressed on me the power of focus, as well as shared valuable business tools. My third coach, Alissa, helped me to become a better coach myself through tools and insights she shared.

However, while it is extremely impactful, coaching is not affordable for everyone. Fortunately, there are several options beyond individual coaching that can provide significant incremental progress toward one's goals, whether those goals relate to job performance, health, or personal growth.

Accountability and support are essential to success in any life area. Therefore, I recommend that everyone have a personal "board of directors"—a support network of positive people who will hold you accountable for maintaining focus and moving forward in your goals. Stephen Covey said, "Accountability breeds response-ability." There is something about knowing that you will have to answer to someone that motivates you to complete a task. Following are seven ways to develop your own board of directors, so that you can get moving in the right direction in ways that are affordable to any budget. Personally, I need a *lot* of accountability, so I have used all of these tactics:

1. **Join a coaching group.** Group coaching is a more reasonably priced option than individual coaching. It provides great insights, tools, and guidance from the coach, along with an opportunity for additional perspectives from fellow group members. Look for a group with a similar focus to yours and one small enough to allow personal interaction from each group member.

2. **Get a mentor.** A mentor is someone who will give advice, share resources, and introduce you to people who can help you move forward in your career. Reach out to someone who is doing well in his or her field or in the field you want to go into and request a small amount of time. This relationship should develop naturally over time and can be formal or informal.

3. **Start a Mastermind group.** A Mastermind group is an alliance of like-minded, achievement-oriented individuals who meet

to leverage each other's success. Participants raise the bar by challenging each other to create and implement goals, brainstorm ideas, and support each other with total honesty, respect, and compassion. Mastermind participants act as catalysts for growth—you are each other's biggest critics and strongest supporters. The group should consist of three to six people who are goal focused and will give you honest feedback and practical advice. Iron sharpens iron.

4. **Get an accountability partner.** An accountability partner is someone who will encourage you to achieve your goals while holding your feet to the fire. Preferably not a close friend or family member, your accountability partner should be someone who will give you honest feedback and suggestions, and who will not allow you to make excuses for nonperformance. Set a weekly schedule to check in with your accountability partner.

5. **Declare integrity days.** An integrity day is a day when you and at least one other person check in at regular intervals to account for progress toward your goals. At the

beginning of each time block, each person gives a report of his or her progress during the last time block and states what will be focused on during the next time block. The check-ins should only take 30 seconds to one minute per person, so that it does not distract from anyone's productivity.

6. **Invest in professional development.** Be a lifelong learner. Invest in yourself and continue to grow your skills by reading relevant books, attending workshops and conferences, and joining professional organizations.

7. **Expand your network.** Connect with like-minded people who can share information, contacts, and ideas. Network for quality, not quantity. Focus on building relationships that will be mutually beneficial through in-person networking events, volunteer organizations, and professional online forums such as LinkedIn. Look to give as well as to get—offer assistance to others so that people begin to recognize your value. Always follow up within 48 hours of initial contact to explore any synergies that you might have identified.

If you ever get stuck in a rut, lose focus while working toward your goals, or just need another point of view, be sure to enlist the aid of your team members. Whether your goals are personal or professional, taking accountability and utilizing a support team will give you the clarity and momentum you need to succeed. I'd like to challenge you to create your personal board of directors in order to accelerate your path to achievement. And while you are moving along that path, remember to reach back and mentor someone else along the way.

LESSON #51

BEATING THE BLUES

"Develop an attitude of gratitude, and give thanks for everything that happens to you, knowing that every step forward is a step toward achieving something bigger and better than your current situation."

BRIAN TRACY

It happens at the end of the year, every year—the time for hors d'oeuvres eating, eggnog drinking, and overall holiday cheer. Unfortunately, many people feel that something is lacking in their lives even in the midst of all the merriment. For some, the year's end leads to the holiday blues as they reflect on the past year and the things they might not have accomplished—the promotion they didn't get, the pounds they didn't lose, the relationship that fell apart, the house they couldn't afford, the resolutions they didn't stick to. (What did I tell you about New Year's resolutions?) For a while, I used to get those blues every year.

While it is easy to focus on the "should haves," it is much better to focus on the future. There is a lot that you can do during the last few days of the year—while you're on vacation or when the office is quiet—to set up for the coming year and lay plans for it to be your best year ever. The first step to moving forward is to be able to look back with appreciation, rather than regret. During those times of reflection, acknowledge and appreciate the blessings of health, friendship, family, food, and shelter.

To close out the year (or even each day) on a positive note, do this exercise to release the negative energy and create the right environment for success. List the things, from *a* to *z,* that you are grateful for. Here are some ideas to get you started:

A The *air* that flows through your lungs daily without you even thinking about it. The ability to breathe clean air is often taken for granted. Many people live in toxic environments and do not have access to clean air. Others have respiratory issues that cause health concerns. If you are able to breathe without concern, be grateful for that capability.

B Your daily *bread.* Few Americans have the problem of wondering where their next meal will come from. In fact, most of us have the opposite problem—we ingest an abundance of food, often to our physical detriment. Take the time to consider those who are less fortunate and perhaps to engage in a short fast to detoxify your body and strengthen your spirit.

C Your steadfast *courage.* Many of you have faced things that would have made others cower in fear. Yet, with faith and courage, you persevere through the storms of life, knowing that going through a valley means you will come out, stronger, on the other side.

Continue your list until you have written something for each letter of the alphabet (feel free to check the dictionary for help with *q* and *z*). You'll find that focusing more on your "haves" and less on your "have-nots" will make you more appreciative of what you have been blessed with.

The end of each year, or even the end of each season of your life, should be a time of reflection, of giving thanks, and for looking forward to a fresh new start. Each new year or new season provides a clean slate with new opportunities and a chance for greater focus on your goals. Author William Arthur Ward said, "Feeling gratitude and not expressing it is like wrapping a present and not giving it." The more we consciously give thanks for what we have, the more we open ourselves up to receive.

ENVISION A NEW BEGINNING

"The beginning is the most important part of the work."

PLATO, ANCIENT GREEK PHILOSOPHER

Are you living your life by design or by accident? Thomas Edison said, "If we did all the things we are capable of doing, we would literally astonish ourselves." Most of us know there is more that we want to achieve in our lives, but often we do not know where to begin.

Over the past several years, I have created mental and written plans for most of the goals that I really wanted to achieve. Even before I realized the power of having a strong vision, I was calling things into my life by having a clear mental picture of what I wanted and by preparing myself to receive it. My favorite book says, "Write the vision; make it plain." I didn't know that when I created a mental picture of teaching on the college level, I'd have opportunities to teach at three schools dropped into my lap, one after the other. I didn't know when I wrote out the topics and guests for my desired radio show that I'd actually be contacted, out of the blue, by the general manager of a radio station who would offer me my own show. I could go on to talk about landing the publishing deal for this book and even more examples. Popularized in recent years by the book and movie called *The Secret,* the power of the Law of Attraction has become more understood. We attract what we focus on. However, we still have to do the work, so that we're ready when the opportunity presents itself.

Think about your goals and dreams. What are the various areas of your life in which you'd like to see major changes? Is it your relationships? Your finances? Your career or business? Your lifestyle? Every so often, I like to revisit my goals to make sure that (a) I still want the same things and (b) I'm on track to achieve what I set my sights on. Each day brings another opportunity to review our goals and to make a fresh start.

Imagine a perfect day in your life five years from now. What does it look like and feel like? Who are you sharing that day with? Where are you living and vacationing? How is your health? Once you have a clear picture of your desired life, how do you transform your desires into definite goals that you can attain?

As I've mentioned, I believe that one of the best ways to create the necessary focus in your life to achieve your goals is to create a vision board. A vision board allows you to create a picture of the future that you envision for yourself. I like to focus on various life areas, both together and separately. Therefore, I create multiple vision boards for lifestyle, business, relationships, and health. My business vision board includes my business goals and the positive impact that I'd like to have on the lives of other people, empowering them to reach their highest potential. My lifestyle vision board includes my goals related to health, relationships, finances, and so on. My relationship and healthy eating vision boards focus more specifically on those areas.

It is said that a picture is worth a thousand words. What makes pictures so powerful? Visual images evoke strong feelings that influence our thoughts and behavior, even when we are not aware of it; they work on us on a deeper level than rational thought. Advertisers know this; they have become adept at combining words and pictures and adding just a bit of music . . . Next thing we know, we are buying things we didn't even know we needed!

I once heard of a study on creative visualization in sports, where Olympic athletes were trained with various combinations of physical training and visualization. The athletes who used more visualization performed better in the Olympics. To become a winner, you have to first think like one.

211

What if you were able to harness the same power used by Madison Avenue and by the Olympic athletes to create the future you desire? You can. Creating a vision board, with words and pictures that portray your desired future, will help you clarify your vision and inspire you to take the necessary actions to fulfill that vision. The subconscious mind cannot tell the difference between what we think is happening and what is really happening. So, if you can begin to internalize the feelings of success that accompany the accomplishment of your goals, your subconscious mind will propel your body to complete the needed steps to get there. Just as the researchers discovered in the case of the Olympic athletes, mental images can act as a prelude to muscular impulses.

For example, I hate working out, but when I have a strong vision of how I will look and feel once I achieve my fitness goals, I find myself waking up earlier than usual with the thought, *Well, I'm awake. I might as well get up and work out.*

Here are some examples of how you can incorporate visualization into your life and goals:

- **If you're buying a new house, see yourself walking through your new house.** Who is walking with you? See each room as you want it to look. Imagine the smells as you walk through the kitchen, the garden, and so on.

- **If you're a golfer, feel yourself hitting the golf ball 250 yards straight across the fairway.** Feel your buddies slap you on the back as you sink the winning putt.

- **If a new car is what you desire, see yourself sitting behind the wheel of your new car—the exact year, model, and color you want.** Feel the steering wheel. Smell the leather. Feel the car gliding as you drive down the streets, waving at neighbors as you pull into your parking space.

It is all within your reach if you can visualize it strongly enough.

How Do You Make a Vision Board?

Gather pictures and words from magazines, books, or the Internet that have a strong impact on you and represent what you desire to see in your life (a new business or career, love, a new home, travel, your ideal weight, and so on). You will also need scissors, glue, colored paper, poster board, and mirrors or pictures of yourself. I like to put my name and picture on bestseller lists, conference speaker lists, and other places I'd like to see myself in the future.

What Are the Benefits of a Vision Board?

- **It creates focus.** Having a visual representation of the life you want will keep you focused on achieving it.

- **It's fun.** Who doesn't love dreaming? Who doesn't love going through a favorite magazine and ripping things out?

- **It's flexible.** As your life changes, so can your vision board. As you reach new goals, you can take images off. And as you create new dreams for yourself, you can add pictures.

How Can You Use Your Vision Board?

- **Put your board where you will see it.** Have it in your field of vision so you will be inspired to act on it. Only through repeated visualization of your goals can you begin to make your dreams a reality. Review your board often and see what manifests itself.

- **Use your board to help determine your next steps in life.** Does what you're planning to do fit with your overall life vision?

- **Use your board to change your mood.** When you feel down, look at your board and get inspired.

- **Use your board to give thanks for what is to come.** Giving thanks opens us up to receive even more.

Life is largely a matter of action and expectation. You must expect success and take action. The dreams you believe in *can* become a reality. Set your goals high, and create a new vision for your life. Set high expectations and take action now, and you'll succeed beyond your wildest expectations!

LEAVE YOUR MARK

*"I am only one, but I am one. I can't do everything,
but I can do something. The something I ought to do,
I can do. And by the grace of God, I will."*

EDWARD EVERETT HALE,
AMERICAN CLERGYMAN AND WRITER

Growing up, I heard the above quote used many times by my father. My dad was an outgoing sort; he made friends easily and loved to laugh and joke. Often people would remark on how he was the first person to make them feel welcome on the job or at church. That is not a bad thing to be known for.

Most of us want to be remembered for something we've done. No one wants to go through life feeling that the world would be no different if they were not in it. Some people make a difference through science, others through community activism, entertainment, and so on. Whatever your gift is, put it into play.

As I was out walking one day, I noticed that a couple of graffiti artists had been pretty busy. It was only a small, simple one-color design, but they'd left "tags" to identify themselves. I wondered who the artists were and what motivated them to do this—was it the desire to create art or the desire for attention? I wished I knew who they were so I could talk to them. They obviously wanted to share something of themselves with the world. It was clear that they were passionate about their art, because they wanted it to be seen. I couldn't help but wonder how that skill and passion could be better utilized to impact more people and actually earn the artists a living. Could they channel that energy into something that would make the world a better place? Would they even be interested in doing that? I just wanted to talk to them to get to the bottom of it all.

What difference are you making in the lives of others with your gifts? How are you using your skills, aptitudes, and personality to impact other people? Are you using them selfishly, just for personal gratification, or are you channeling them in a way that will leave a lasting legacy?

Often when people think about leaving a mark, they think about how they can impact the world. It doesn't take that much to leave a mark. If just one life is touched in a positive way by something you've done, you have made a difference. It might be your children or someone in your family who is looking for direction. It could be someone you mentor or a stranger who needs temporary assistance. Your mark doesn't have to extend across the globe; it can be across your household or across your neighborhood. Just know that the important thing is to share your gifts and talents whenever you have the opportunity.

Don't Get Caught Unaware . . .

"The secret of success in life is for a man to be ready for his opportunity when it comes."

Benjamin Disraeli

The announcement had been hanging in the lobby of my condo building for more than two weeks, but somehow I forgot that morning. So, when there was a knock on my door just after 9 A.M., I had no idea who it was. Usually, I am not one to stay in bed late, but of course that morning I was not dressed and had to throw on something—anything—very quickly to answer the door. The exterminator had arrived for our building's annual spraying.

My condo was not a pretty sight. I'd been working on my taxes, so papers were all over the floor. I'd washed my hair the night before, and all my hair stuff—shampoo, conditioner, blow-dryer, flat iron, curling iron, and so on—was on my vanity. And, on top of all that, I was speaking at an event that day, so the night before I'd decided to figure out what I was going to wear (like I ever do that). So all the clothes and shoes I'd tried on were *everywhere.* It was just a hot mess!

The door to the second bedroom, which was actually clean, was closed, so the exterminator didn't go in there. He probably thought the door was closed because that room was even worse. I am still feeling so embarrassed just thinking about it (I can't believe I'm sharing this story). I was mortified when he left as I began to walk through the rooms, reliving everything that he saw.

That was a real lesson to me about the importance of being ready. Whether it is a professional opportunity, a financial challenge, a relationship, or something that requires physical stamina, preparation will save us from embarrassment and help us to put our best foot forward in any situation.

I determined then that no one would ever see my home looking that way again, even if they caught me off guard. And that lesson also encouraged me to be sure that I'm prepared for other situations, as well. Preparation is definitely the secret to success—and to avoiding embarrassment!

AVOID TOO MUCH OF A GOOD THING

"Why then, can one desire too much of a good thing?"
WILLIAM SHAKESPEARE, *AS YOU LIKE IT*

I was walking through the exhibit hall of a women's conference and there was a booth where medical staff had some sort of contraption that tested the antioxidant levels of those who were willing to stop and surrender their finger. Ultimately, the goal was to sell you on the products they were promoting to raise your antioxidant levels. When they tested mine, no one could believe how high my levels were— much higher than anyone else's they'd measured (including themselves) and almost off their chart. Trying to get to the bottom of it, the doctor asked me a barrage of questions: "Do you drink red wine?" "Green tea?" "Eat a lot of berries?"

"You must eat a lot of green vegetables . . . legumes?" It went on. The answer to every question they asked was no.

Of course, they still tried to sell me their products. As I walked away, I realized the answer: dark chocolate. They say that dark chocolate is very high in antioxidants and good for you in moderation. However, I tend to go a bit beyond moderation in my consumption of it. The high antioxidant levels gained by eating dark chocolate can easily be overshadowed by an equally high waist circumference, which can cause its own set of issues.

There are certain things we all love that are extremely good for us in reasonable amounts. However, we sometimes let our natural enjoyment of things get out of control. The word *temperance* means that we should practice moderation in all things, even those things that are good. We should be able to control our urges and habits, not let them control us.

How can something that is essentially good for us end up being so bad for us? In most things, there is a danger of excess. It is definitely possible to have too much of a good thing.

Water is good for our bodies, our crops, and our flowers. Humans are composed of 70 percent water, and if we allow our bodies to become dehydrated, we can suffer serious consequences, even death. However, water can be a harmful and devastating force if it gets out of control.

For example, in the December 2004 tsunami in Southeast Asia, by some estimates, more than 200,000 people lost their lives. Not only were lives lost because of the flood, but thousands were affected by residual diseases, such as dengue fever, malaria, and mental disorders. Many orphaned children and displaced families are still attempting to rebuild their lives after the loss of homes and loved ones.

Exposure to the sun provides the critical vitamin D needed by our bodies better than any man-made vitamin can. In addition to being good for our skin, hair, and nails, healthy doses of vitamin D have been shown to reduce risk of certain cancers, heart disease, autoimmune diseases, type 1 diabetes, and muscle and bone pain. However, it has also been proven that too much sun exposure can lead to skin cancer.

It goes without saying that we need food to survive. Healthy servings of fruits and vegetables at the core of our diets will give us all the nutrients we need. However, too much food, especially of the wrong types, can lead to obesity, type 2 diabetes, heart disease, stroke, and osteoporosis. Our excessive portion sizes have gotten out of control. Using the terminology of a popular restaurant chain, we supersize everything. We have learned to alter healthy food from the manner in which it was intended to be eaten. We take fresh greens, full of vitamins and without fat, and we put pork on them and load them up with salt. We take a fresh, crisp apple, take off the nutrient-rich peel, and then layer it with sugar, butter, and dough to make a pie.

E-mail and text messaging are great ways to communicate in a world where everyone is moving quickly in different directions. However, overrelying on these methods can impede our ability to communicate face-to-face. It can also greatly increase the probability of miscommunication.

There is even such a thing as too much sleep. While the average adult should have six to seven hours of sleep per night, many people sleep much longer than they need and end up feeling sluggish the next day, not to mention the opportunities they miss out on while they are in a vegetative state. I have a good friend who loves to sleep late when she gets the opportunity. She once told another friend and me of a time when she went to visit relatives and was so tired that she slept for 13 hours before one of the children in the family insisted on waking her up. One of the popular department stores in Chicago periodically has a 13-hour sale. We tease her now, telling her that she would miss the sale because she would be asleep!

More is not necessarily better. A bigger house means a bigger mortgage (and more to clean). More credit leads to more debt, not only in our personal lives but in our economy, as evidenced by the recent subprime mortgage crisis.

Children who are spoiled with too many material things often end up being irresponsible adults.

Sometimes it is better to simplify our lives and live with a bit less. It frees up our time and energy to focus on what really matters. I have learned that a flexible schedule is more important to me than a high salary, so I focus on doing things I enjoy to make money, rather than working a 60-hour week at a job I do not enjoy. Look for ways to scale back in those areas of life where you might be tempted to overindulge. I think you'll find that the simple life is no less enjoyable.

SOMETIMES YOU JUST KNOW . . .

"I'll know it when I see it."

AMERICAN COLLOQUIALISM

A couple of years ago, I was given a ticket to an author event that was a costume ball. Not having dressed in a costume for many years, I wasn't too excited about the prospect of having to do so. I would have to purchase a costume, because the ones I kept in storage were so old (dry rot could be an issue) and probably didn't fit anymore. Besides, I prefer spending my money on outfits that I can get a bit more practical use out of.

I contemplated not going, but I decided that it would be rude not to use the ticket. The woman who invited me was so supportive of authors and had shared many helpful tips with me in the past. Besides, Kiela had purchased a ticket and wanted to go, so I had to get something to-gether. I decided to go the least expensive route and went with my friend Denise to some thrift stores. Halloween was approaching, and I was expecting that costumes would be fairly plentiful. I was right, but I didn't see anything that I remotely liked (witches and ghouls—boring!). As soon as we walked into the next store, I saw it. There was no doubt in my mind what my costume would be—a Hershey's Kiss! (As I've said, my love for chocolate runs deep.)

The costume consisted of a silver, puffy kiss-shaped dress and a matching kiss-shaped hat complete with a white tassel that read, "Hershey's Kiss." I was so excited! I was done looking and had a great costume. I wore it with white tights and silver sandals, and, yes, I do have pictures thanks to my neighbor across the hall, who could barely hold the camera still for laughing at my outfit.

Fast forward to the event . . . When I walked into the party—late, of course, for those who know me—everyone was whispering and staring. I started to get nervous, until I heard what they were saying: "That's so cute." "Hershey's Kiss . . . I love it!" I smiled and thought, *I think I got this!* At the end of the event, with about 200 people all competing in the costume contest, guess who took first prize? Yeah, sometimes you just know it's right.

I'm sure there have been times in your life where you've had a gut feeling about something, be it good or bad. Was it a job prospect? Travel plans? A romantic re-lationship? We often second-guess ourselves instead of trusting our first instincts. There are definitely a couple of relationships that I would have passed on if I'd trusted my gut. I know someone who knew on her wedding day that she was making the wrong decision. In the end, it turned out she was right. Even when taking a test, they say that the first answer you think of is usually the correct one. I recall changing a right answer to a wrong one because I overthought a problem on a physics test in college. I'm sure it's happened many times, but I remember mentally kicking myself over that one. It's good to pay attention to our intuition.

Have you ever felt that instinctive feeling in a posi-tive way? Have you ever immediately known that you were making the right decision? Isn't it a great feeling to have? Whether it is an outfit, a relationship, or a business deci-sion, it feels good to know that you're on the right track.

When you really do know you're on the right track, it's important to act on what you're feeling. If not, you could miss an opportunity that was right there waiting for you. Opportunities are all around us, but it is up to us to act on them and bring what we want into fruition. I'm sure glad I didn't leave that costume in the store.

LESSON #57

IDENTIFY
THE ENEMY

"Underachiever and proud of it."
BART SIMPSON (ON A T-SHIRT)

Okay, I know I shouldn't have polished off the rest of that bag of dark chocolate–covered almonds. I really do want to look good in that swimsuit I bought last week before I go on my next vacation. But I needed something to give me a quick boost while I'm writing. I'll get on the treadmill tomorrow. Sound familiar? I'm just as guilty of it as anyone else (I honestly did just eat the rest of the bag). We make bad decisions; then, we justify them to make ourselves feel better. Or maybe we simply promise to do better in the future.

Years ago, the famous cartoonist Walt Kelly wrote the immortal quote for his character, Pogo Possum: "We have met the enemy and he is us." When it comes to our goals and dreams, we often turn out to be our own worst enemies. The true enemy could be called "inner me." Once we get rid of our self-defeating practices, we have won half the battle. To follow Sun Tzu's advice in *The Art of War,* if you know your enemy, it allows you to outsmart and defeat him. Applying that same principle, knowing ourselves will allow us to defeat the self-sabotaging patterns that we have followed over and over leading to unsuccessful outcomes.

Are you always late for work, then wonder why you always get passed over for a promotion?

Do you stock up on junk food at the supermarket, then wonder why you can't fit into your skinny jeans?

Is your shopping habit causing your credit card bills to spiral out of control?

In order to change our patterns, we must rethink the ways we've been doing things. We must apply new standards to our lives in order to get new outcomes. After all, you cannot make a different dress using the same old pattern. As the saying goes, "If you do what you've always done, you'll get what you always got."

What are some ways that we hold ourselves back from living up to our full potential?

- **Autopilot.** Sometimes we have a tendency to just let things happen in our lives.

We go through life reacting rather than responding. We become thermometers, reflecting what is going on around us ("I had a bad day." "I'm depressed."), rather than thermostats regulating our environment ("Today was a rough day. I think I'll call a friend and go out to dinner so I can have some fun."). Focus on how you can change your attitude and then your behavior so you can control your environment rather than it controlling you. Practice making decisions that will move you forward in a positive direction rather than accepting whatever outcome is presented to you.

- **Negative self-talk.** In addition to sometimes being our own worst enemies, we are also our own worst critics. From our physical features to our intelligence to our bank accounts, we're always finding something wrong with ourselves. Focus on the positives and learn to appreciate all the good things about yourself, from your wonderful character traits to your strong work ethic, and be sure to include those physical features, as well.

- **Fear.** We often worry so much about the future that we set ourselves up for failure before we even try. Break through the barrier of fear that is holding you back from achieving your goals. Think about where you are now and where you really want to be. Draw a line down the middle of a sheet of paper. On the left side, write down all the negative things that can happen if you move forward toward one of your goals. On the right side, write down all the positive things that can happen if you move forward toward that same goal. Which side has the most entries? If I were a betting woman, I'd wager that there is more on the right side. And if that is the case, what is stopping you from moving forward toward the desires of your heart?

- **Procrastination.** We all like to put off unpleasant tasks. The problem with that is they are always there, hanging over our heads. I absolutely hate doing expense reports for the contract I'm working on. But guess what? If I don't do them, I won't get paid. Housecleaning isn't my favorite task, either, but I know what will happen if I just let it go. Think about the consequences that you will incur for putting things off that you know need to be done. Will things get better or worse as a result of the delay?

- **Unforgiveness.** Sometimes we beat ourselves up over and over about the same things. It seems to be more difficult to forgive ourselves than it is to forgive others who have wronged us. Learning to forgive yourself is the first step on the journey to peace. Release it and move on.

Some habits might seem harmless, but, after a while, repeating the same negative behaviors can damage our attitudes and our progress toward our goals. Let go of habits that are no longer serving you.

Ask for honest feedback from a few friends or family members who love you enough to be honest but kind. No one likes criticism, but sometimes feedback from others will help us to recognize our own destructive behaviors.

We need to destroy the negative patterns that keep us repeating the same mistakes over and over. Do not stay for years in a frustrating and unfulfilling job for fear of not paying the bills. Find a new job while you're on your old job and keep moving ahead. Do not move forward in a damaging relationship out of fear of not having another choice or chance. Value yourself enough to know that there is someone out there who will appreciate what you bring to the table.

We should learn not only from the bad choices we make, but also from the mistakes of others to avoid making them ourselves. In that way, we can move from being our own worst enemies to being our own best friends.

MANAGE YOUR PRIORITIES, NOT YOUR TIME

"It's not enough to be industrious; so are the ants.
What are you industrious about?"

HENRY DAVID THOREAU

Okay, let's see . . . Went to the grocery store. Check. Stopped at the cleaners. Check. Reviewed the proposal to make sure the most up-to-date information was included. Check. The list goes on. We spend our days checking a lot of things off the "list," then turn the lights off at night exhausted but unfulfilled. We do so many things during the course of a day, but how many of them are really linked to our true values and goals?

I'm sure you know someone whose story might sound like this: Brenda wanted to become the top salesperson in her company. She decided to examine the habits of successful salespeople she knew to see what activities made them successful. *Hmm,* she thought. *They work twelve hours a day, six or seven days a week. If it worked for them, I guess that's what I should do.* So, she gave up a large portion of her leisure time in her quest for financial success. Things went well for a while. But as time went on, Brenda felt a growing sense of unease. She couldn't understand why working toward her goal made her so miserable. The problem was, Brenda's goal didn't support her true values. She was being busy about the wrong things. Brenda's priority had always been spending time with her family and friends, but she now made her work her main priority. She was sacrificing what mattered to her most.

I've been there, and I'm sure you have, as well. People often focus on time management, when what we really need to manage is our priorities, making sure they are aligned with what we truly value. If we want to live authentically, we must focus less on managing our time and more on managing our priorities. If you eliminate actions and habits that don't align with your true priorities, the time crunch will take care of itself.

If you encounter resistance while attempting to reach certain goals or perform certain tasks, chances are you're doing something you really don't want to do, something that is not consistent with your deepest values.

We want to be there for the important people in our lives, but often our support of others is detrimental to our own success. Most of us have done things that we didn't want to do or didn't have time to do simply because someone asked or expected us to do it. Just because a task is important to someone else doesn't mean it has to be the number one priority in your life. Ask yourself if you are fulfilling a job because it is valuable to you, or if it is because it is what *someone else* expects of you. Then decide how your time would best be spent. You'll see how much more time and energy you'll have when you focus on managing your priorities, not your time.

ALONE DOES NOT MEAN LONELY

"Born not from our flesh, but born in our hearts, you were longed for and wanted and loved from the start."

UNKNOWN

Here I am, once again, returning to an empty house. This was often the thought on Janice's mind as she headed to her three-bedroom house. She'd had a meeting after work, as she did most days of the week, so it was already late in the evening. She juggled a bag of groceries as she turned the key in her door. Janice had gone grocery shopping, in a way, to postpone going home to an empty house. Feelings of loneliness and despair gripped her as she set the groceries on the kitchen counter. Janice longed to be greeted by someone when she walked in the door, who would tell her they'd missed her and share their day's adventures with her. She wanted someone to welcome her home, wrap loving arms around her, and share a home-cooked meal.

I have heard many professional, single women talk about the loneliness they feel when they return to their big, beautiful homes at the end of a stressful workday and no one is there to greet them. I also know married people who feel this way because they feel their family is not complete without children. Fortunately, there are many ways to decrease the loneliness in our lives. All it takes is a little creative thinking.

If you are at all feeling like the above scenario, here are some suggestions for alleviating these emotions:

- **Join an organization.** Find one that meets your personal or professional interests. I've found, over the years, that there really is an organization for everything, so if you're looking to connect with single bricklayers who like the color green, I'm sure there's a club for that.

- **Become a mentor.** There are formal programs, like Big Brothers Big Sisters, but you could also connect with a young person who needs either professional or personal guidance through organizations or through people you already know.

- **Adopt a pet from a shelter.** There are thousands of furry companions who would welcome a loving home and who would literally dance with joy when you returned home each evening.

- **Volunteer at a nursing home.** If you think you're lonely, imagine those who might be even more so. Many nursing home residents do not have visitors, and it would mean a lot to have someone to spend time with— someone who they know will return to see them again and again. Not only would the residents appreciate your attention, but it would give great relief to the workers to have additional hands and hearts on deck.

- **Adopt a child.** I have friends, both married and single, who have chosen to adopt children or to raise foster children, and it has changed their lives in ways that are indescribable. The love and joy they give to their children and receive in return has changed their lives forever. Their sacrifices are met with much appreciation, especially from the children who were old enough to know what their lives were like before they had a real home.

When we speak of relationships, most people's minds go directly to romantic relationships, but there are many types of relationships that can add happiness and fulfillment to our lives. There is always room for additional love, so why not add someone to the list of people you can love and share your life with?

DON'T GET STUCK IN THE MEANTIME

"We are set in our ways, bound by our perspectives, and stuck in our thinking."

JOEL OSTEEN

What do we do while we're waiting to get from here to there? What do we do between now and then? What is happening while we're waiting for what is supposed to happen in our lives?

We've all been there. You know there's something you're supposed to be doing with your life. But you're not sure exactly what it is. "So," we say to ourselves, "I might as well just hang out here in the meantime . . ."

Whether it has been a job, a relationship, or a home, we have spent time in situations that we knew were just temporary until the right thing came along. Sometimes we've even fooled ourselves into thinking that where we were—that comfort zone—was the right place for us. We have all tried to shave the edges off some square pegs in order to fit them into round holes. There is something about those meantime periods that keep us engaged. Let's face it: they can be pretty attractive at times. However, there is also something about the meantime period that we know is an ultimate deal breaker.

Meantime periods help pass the time while we are still searching for our passion and purpose. Unfortunately, they also waste valuable time. Meantime periods are often merely filling in the emotional—and sometimes physical—gaps that are present when we seek temporary fulfillment. We can never move to where we really want and deserve to be in life as long as we are stuck in a meantime period.

When we are in a meantime period, we sometimes allow feelings to overrule logic and common sense. However, our intuition rarely leads us astray. If we are picking up a vibe that something is not right, usually something is not right. If you're feeling that way, trust the signals and move on. Do not hold on to hope when all the signs indicate that you should cut your losses.

Sometimes we pour good money after bad into a business that is just not working. We spend years in a relationship that is not going anywhere. We keep taking that old beater to the car repair shop instead of just cutting our losses and buying a new one.

We have all had meantime periods, and some of them were effective for our growth and our transitions in life. If we learn something valuable while we're in the Land of Meantime, we will grow from it and hopefully avoid a similar situation in the future. The problem is that some of us are drawn to the same situations over and over again. Here's a hint: If you start to see a pattern, whether it is in personal relationships, business, health, or whatever, look for the common denominator. If that's you, recognize that it is time to make some different choices in life. As the opening suggests, if you see that the sun is moving, don't stay in the same place. The earth is constantly moving. Change your direction and move with it!

LESSON #61

WHAT DO YOU WORSHIP?

*"Every one of us is, even from his mother's womb,
a master craftsman of idols."*

JOHN CALVIN

I travel to an annual conference with friends every year. In addition to conference workshops and parties, our Chicago group always manages to sightsee, experience local cuisine, and, most importantly for the women in the group, shop! Jewelry has always been a passion for some of us, and we add to our assortment with almost every trip. Not only do we love to accumulate it, but we bring a sizable portion of our collections with us when we travel.

Several years ago, we were returning from the conference, and, as is our custom, we had overpacked. However, uncharacteristically, we managed to get to the airport

245

exceptionally early for our flight. Feeling pretty proud of ourselves for that feat, we checked our bags and waited for our flight to board. In my determination to lighten my carry-on items, I'd checked the suitcase that contained my large jewelry roll. It wasn't until after we'd cleared security that I realized I'd forgotten to lock it (this was pre-9/11, when luggage could still be locked). *Oh, well,* I thought. *No big deal.* I'm sure you can see where this is going . . .

On the plane, my friend Gwen and I reviewed our jewelry purchases from the trip. We chatted on and on about how we'd built up our collections over the years and how we'd bought things from all over in our travels—definitely an irreplaceable assortment. We were both feeling pretty proud of what we'd amassed over the years. I pointed out that I was wearing my favorite piece at the time—a pair of dangling black Mayan-inspired earrings, purchased just the night before. Finally, we moved to other subjects.

As you've probably guessed, when I arrived home and began unpacking, my jewelry roll was nowhere to be found. Our early arrival at the airport had given some unscrupulous airport employee plenty of time to rummage through my unlocked bag. My grief was palpable. I've always felt that I had a pretty level head when it comes to "things"—I never got upset about dents or scratches on my car, for example. "It is just a car," I'd say magnanimously. "It's replaceable." But I found the loss of all my favorite jewelry to be much more difficult to deal with. I'm not much of a crier, but if I were, I'm sure this would've been a time to take advantage of a good cry. I'd traveled all over to collect those pieces, so replacing them would be next to impossible. And they had so much sentimental value—they triggered wonderful memories of trips with my girlfriends. I couldn't re-create those memories. I called the airline to report the loss. I prayed. And nothing worked. My priceless (costume) jewelry was still gone. I was heartbroken.

It was about that time that I realized that I was attaching way too much importance to that jewelry. Had I exalted my jewelry to the level of a god? I felt guilty for attaching so much importance to something that was only a thing. A few years after that incident, I realized that I still struggled with the jewelry idol when, in a single day, I lost two earrings. One was inexpensive and easily replaceable. I handled that loss in admirable fashion. However, when I realized that I had lost one of a pair from a very expensive set, I was distraught. I retraced my steps from the car to the house. I called the restaurant where my friends and I had eaten that night. I remembered hearing something drop at one point during the evening, and I mentally kicked myself for only glancing down to see if I'd dropped something. How could I have been so careless?

My mother thought in black and white, and she always spoke her mind. She wasted no time in reminding me that it was just an *earring*. I grudgingly admitted that she was right. Life is a constant process of growth, and it is a blessing to have people in our lives who can help us stay grounded and recognize the areas where we need to improve.

When we examine the story of the Israelites who, on their release from slavery in ancient Egypt, immediately began to doubt God, we might think of how shortsighted they must have been to have forgotten everything He had done for them up to that point—the whole Red Sea parting, cloud by day, fire by night, manna from heaven thing. You'd think those types of experiences would stick with a person for a while! But as soon as God's physical presence was no longer in view, they decided to create an image that they could see and worship, instead of focusing on all the blessings and miracles they'd received from God. Were they really that much different than we are today?

Like the ancient Israelites, I had created my own idol. True, I didn't melt it down and make a golden (or, in this case, gold-plated) calf, but I worshipped it nonetheless. We can attach so much importance to insignificant things like jewelry, houses, power, or prestige that we put them ahead of the basic blessings of faith, family, health, friendship, and shelter. We lose sight of what is really important in our lives.

I challenge you to examine whether there are any "idols" that you might be putting ahead of the people who should be receiving your love and attention. If there are, reposition them so that you are devoting your time and affection to what is really most important in the long run.

LESSON #62

PICK YOUR FRIENDS CAREFULLY

"Life is partly what we make it, and partly what it is made by the friends we choose."

TEHYI HSIEH

There is a saying that goes, "Show me your five closest friends, and I'll show you exactly who you are." There is a lot of truth in the belief that we are who we associate with. What you feed your mind on, you become. If you associate with positive people, you will have a more positive attitude. If you associate with smokers, you will most likely become one. And if you associate with overspenders, chances are you probably overspend right alongside them.

There comes a time when it becomes necessary to review your base of friends and associates to see which of them are still on the same path you are traveling. If your goal is to excel in business, science, sports, or any other arena, and your closest friends still don't have their own ambitions, it might be time to expand your friendship base. That is not to say that you can no longer be friends with your old crowd, but you might want to spend less time with them and more time with people whose goals and dreams are as big as yours. It would even be helpful to try to make friends with people who are already more successful than you in your area of focus. Understand that you will not become immediate best friends with these people, because their closest friends will be those like themselves. However, you can learn and make contacts by being around these people, and, as you progress, you'll gain new friendships.

This saying also applies to any other area of your life. Are your closest friends "on the same page" as you when it comes to their spiritual beliefs? Their health—eating and exercise habits? Personal growth? If not, are you sitting on the fence and trying to live in two different worlds? Considering the makeup of human anatomy, "sitting on the fence" for any length of time can become quite uncomfortable. You can shift your weight around, trying to find a more comfortable position, but those spikes at the top will still be mighty painful.

What qualities do your friends possess? Are they qualities you aspire to? Are you seeing loyalty, kindness, compassion, determination, and focus on their goals? Or do your friends demonstrate recklessness, flakiness, jealousy, selfishness, or other negative habits? If the latter, you'd better check your own behavior to see if you are exhibiting the same habits as your friends. It is rare that one person in a group will be vastly different from the rest of the group.

I would encourage you to review your closest associations, as well as your own habits, and determine what changes, if any, need to be made. And if you decide that positive change is needed in your life, invite your friends to join you on your journey.

FIND YOUR NEEDLE IN THE HAYSTACK

"It is never too late to be what you might have been."

GEORGE ELIOT (PEN NAME OF ENGLISH NOVELIST MARY ANN EVANS, 1819–1880)

Some people are so naturally gifted that there is no way that they could *not* clearly identify their life paths—those are the Beethovens and da Vincis of the world. However, many people spend their lives wondering exactly where they fit in. They wonder what their contribution to society should be and spend years trying different things to see what makes them feel fulfilled.

I believe your purpose in life is always tied to your deepest passion. For some, that passion is evident; for others, it is like finding a needle in a haystack. Many of us never sift through all the straws to finally sort out the elusive needle. Short of setting the hay on fire, how do we sort through all the excess to get to what we're really seeking to find—our life purpose?

For me, maybe because I wasn't paying attention, my journey was a bit like sifting through the straw . . .

I discovered my aptitude for writing as a child. Whenever I was angry at a family member, I'd write him or her a letter, detailing the heinous crimes they'd committed against me. My brother dubbed them "hate notes" (he got most of them). I'm sure that the tip of my number two pencil convinced them all to mend their evil ways and now they are successful, well-balanced individuals because of it.

Growing up, I liked to read more than anything. As a child and young adult, I would have rather read than eaten or slept. And I often did. I moved in phases from mysteries to thrillers to romance novels, back to thrillers, then to inspirational and personal growth. I believe the love of reading is what shaped my passion for writing. Think about what you have been passionate about since you were a child.

I remember high school English. It was my straight A subject all four years. In Mr. Little's freshman English class, I wrote a play entitled *The Water in the Gate.* Our assignment was to write a modern-day play based on a traditional play. I chose *The Sword in the Stone.* In my modern-day adaptation, Richard Nixon was King Arthur and Henry Kissinger was Merlin. Everyone in the cabinet had a role. I started writing the play a day or two before it was due and finished it up during class after everyone else had turned theirs in. Mr. Little asked me if I'd written it by myself. I thought, *Didn't you see me back there at my desk trying to finish before the period was over?* But I wasn't going to point that out to him if he hadn't noticed it himself.

In fact, most of my English assignments were done under tight time constraints. I wouldn't work on a paper for days, sometimes weeks, because I didn't have the exact idea that I wanted. I always needed to wait for inspiration—maybe I was having writer's block and didn't realize it; maybe I was just being lazy. Then, once the ideas started flowing, they would come so quickly that my pen could barely keep pace with my thoughts. I habitually completed my compositions for seventh-period English in sixth-period history. And I always got an A or A+ on the assignments. That only happened because writing was a natural skill for me.

Think about your natural talents and aptitudes. We all have them. Whatever your gift is, you'll find that it probably comes easy to you, and, because of that, you likely take it for granted. If you can't identify what you're good at, think about what people often ask you to do. Or ask a family member or friend what you do well. They'll be able to tell you.

So, why didn't I consider being a journalism major so that I could do what I really enjoyed? Because, like many of you lovely readers, I didn't trust my gift. Instead of focusing on what I liked to do, I listened to the well-meaning counselors who told me that engineering was the field to pursue. "That is where the money is, and, as a female, you can write your own ticket," they said. (Ever gotten any really bad advice?) *Duh, okay,* I thought. I didn't have a clue what I wanted to do with my life, so engineering was just as good as anything. (Of course, my mother always encouraged me to get a job at "the bank"—she'd say it as if there were only one.) So, I chose chemical engineering because I liked chemistry. In retrospect, I think it was more the creativity of the experiments (mixing things together and seeing what happened) than the love of science that intrigued me.

Don't get distracted by what is mainstream; focus on what you really love. Don't follow the money; follow your passion and the money will follow.

After three years of struggling as a chemical engineering major, I transferred and decided to try something else. After graduating with a degree in management, I went back to get my MBA. I accepted the first job I was offered just to get back to Chicago and ended up at a bank (score one for Mom). I held several positions at the bank and worked in just about every line of the business. Somehow it happened that, in every position I took, I always ended up getting the writing assignments. Twice I was the newsletter editor. I wrote the training manuals; I wrote the disaster recovery manual; I was the communications chairperson for the employee affinity group I belonged to. And it wasn't just at work. At church, I had a regular column in the monthly newsletter, wrote plays, presented lessons, and so on. People always told me how much they enjoyed my lessons. But they couldn't have enjoyed them as much as I enjoyed writing them. No feeling could match that of gathering research and putting my thoughts on paper. The feeling I would get when writing was like nothing else. Yet, I still didn't recognize it. I would read inspirational books and think, *I can write this stuff.* And now, at the age of—well, that really isn't important, is it?—I'm finally doing what I was born to do.

What is it that gives you that rush? What makes you feel better than anything else when you do it? What gift comes so naturally to you that it shows up in every aspect of your life? Again, if you aren't sure, ask your friends and family. They can probably see it clearly in you.

Once you identify your gift, pledge that you will start to use it right away. The important thing is not *when* you begin to use your gifts, but *that* you begin to use them.

I'm learning that I need to carry a pen and paper (or, more recently, the memo app on my smartphone) with me at all times. So often I have ideas while I'm out, and by the time I get home, I've forgotten them. I get inspired while walking on the lakefront. Once, an hour on the elliptical machine at the gym (something I don't do nearly often enough) was the source of endless inspiration. Of course, by the time I'd finished working out and got home, I couldn't remember a single one of the great Pulitzer Prize–winning gems of wisdom that I'd created in my mind. But I know there will be more ideas to come.

Whatever it is that you are passionate about can truly be your livelihood, not to mention a source of inspiration to those around you. Whether you make the best pound cake or whether you have the best ear to listen to people's problems, whatever you are naturally gifted with should never be taken for granted. Pay attention to your gift and put it into action and it can bless not only you, but those around you, as well.

DON'T QUIT THE RACE

"Fall seven times, stand up eight."

JAPANESE PROVERB

I remember my brother telling the story of how he discovered, while in the sixth grade, that one of the things he could do better than most of the kids within his sphere of influence was run. He was challenged to race someone almost every day, either on the way to school or on the way back. He generally won (and I'm not just saying that because I'm his little sister). The school didn't have an actual track team, so the boys only ran for fun. One day his gym teacher announced that there would be an open track meet to be held at Gately Stadium on the Far South Side of Chicago.

Track and field was not nearly as popular or as lucrative back then as it is now, so his familiarity with the strategies associated with track was extremely limited. In fact, he would be participating in the first track meet he'd have ever seen. The 50-yard dash was his race of choice. When he arrived at Gately Stadium and registered for the "midget boys" 50-yard dash (he was a late bloomer), he couldn't help noticing that many of the other runners were wearing gym shorts and lightweight spiked running shoes. He was wearing jeans and gym shoes. I wasn't there to witness it, but I'm sure he must have stood out like a sore thumb.

When they took the starting line for the first heat, he noticed that some of the runners got into a three-point stance (like football linemen) and one guy had a device he called "starting blocks." My brother just stood up and leaned over to start the race like he always did. Well, he wound up winning his heat. He then won the quarter final, the semifinal, and the final. He had managed to win the first track event he'd ever entered. His friends congratulated him—"You the man, doc" and "You bad, man." (It was a long time ago and they used to say corny stuff like that back then.) Needless to say, he was starting to believe the hype. He decided to enter the mile run. As he surveyed the competition, he became very confident. Nobody in the field *looked* fast to him. He decided that he was going to "turn it out." He was going to be the next Jesse Owens.

As they approached the starting line, he noticed that nobody was doing that silly three-point stance thing. He took that as a good sign. When the gun sounded, he took off. He quickly took the lead and looked around to make sure that he had gotten a good jump on the competition. *I got this,* he thought to himself. Well, you can probably guess what happened after that. Let's fast-forward to the end of the race. As my brother describes it, he *almost* beat the guy who came in next to last! You see, he didn't understand that, as my favorite book says, the race is not given to the strong or the mighty (or the swift), but to he who endures until the end. He didn't realize the mile run was not the same as a sprint and it required a different strategy. The mile run just was not his race. He was a sprinter.

Your race in life—your calling—is unique to you. Don't try to run anyone else's race; just do what you are called to do. If you're a long-distance runner, take your time, watch your breathing, and pace yourself for the long haul. But if you're a sprinter, hit it with all you've got right off the starting block. Whether you win, place, or show is not the point. The point is just to reach the finish line after completing the course.

Marilyn vos Savant said, "Being defeated is often a temporary condition. Giving up is what makes it permanent." Whatever your race and whatever your goal, just keep on running.

LESSON #65

YOUR PASSION WILL INSPIRE OTHERS

"A mediocre idea that generates enthusiasm will go further than a great idea that inspires no one."

MARY KAY ASH

As I've mentioned, my passion for writing began at an early age. By the time I was 14, I knew that I wanted to be an author. However, it took me a while to follow my true calling because I allowed outside influences to shape my thoughts about what I could and should do for a career.

However, after many years in corporate America, I did finally step out and write that first book. My first book sale ever was to a gentleman I met at a networking event. The book was not ready; it was being printed at the time.

However, I was so excited about my upcoming work that I moved from person to person at the event, passing out my homemade bookmarks and cards and telling them that I was an author. I told them all about the premise of the book. Even though it was targeted toward women, in my excitement, I talked about it to everyone I met.

As I discussed the book, a man stopped me and told me that he wanted to buy one. I informed him the book wasn't out yet, but he insisted he wanted to purchase one and asked how much it was. "Fifteen dollars," I replied. He gave me $20 and insisted that I keep the change. I must've been looking at him really strangely by then because he asked, "Do you know why I insisted on buying one of your books?" "No," I said.

The man told me I inspired him because so many people have goals and dreams, yet few people have the courage to follow them. He wanted to buy a book because he wanted to support my dream. That little act of kindness and support meant so much to me.

About four and a half years later, I received an unusual e-mail. It read, "Hi, I'm Nelson. You probably don't remember me, but I was your first book sale." Nelson had run across the makeshift bookmark that I'd made back then and located my e-mail address. He reminded me that he was the one who believed in my dream so much that he wanted to be the first to buy my book. He said,

"It's been a while now and I figure the book should be finished by now, so I'd like to get my autographed copy." He included his address so I could mail him the book. The next day, I was able to finally put that copy of the book in the mail to him.

I still have the $20 bill from my first book sale, kept on my nightstand to remind me that I was indeed able to realize my dream of being an author and that there was someone who believed in me enough to invest in my dream even before it became a reality.

If you believe in the power of your dreams, you will find that there will be others who will believe in you, as well. Where or who your support comes from may surprise you. So, share your big dream (or dreams) with others, and you'll be surprised at the doors that will open for you.

LESSON #66

LOVE IS THICKER THAN BLOOD

"Friends are the family we choose for ourselves."

EDNA BUCHANAN

I feel blessed to have so many friends who are friends for a lifetime. I'm pouting a bit right now because as I'm finishing this book, one segment of said friends is attending an annual professional conference that I usually attend. It was in driving distance, so it became a road trip. Fortunately, they are keeping me up-to-date on the conference activities via text, so that I can hear about what (and who) I'm missing. One friend said that people can't believe she is there without me! I guess at some point, your friends become so close that it is hard to imagine being seen apart from each other.

265

There is a saying that "blood is thicker than water," referring to the strength of family bonds. However, a good friend recently said to me, "love is thicker than blood." In this instance, he was referring to the closeness among our college friends. The bond we share with each other is something no one outside our group can understand. Even with those whom I didn't know during my college years the bond is immediate. It is actually a palpable vibe that others outside our group have both noticed and commented on. And it doesn't matter how long it's been since we've seen each other; the bond remains strong.

I love my family, and I have an awesome one. That, in itself, is a huge blessing, because there are many people who do not have a close relationship with their families. But I also love my "play" families, as well. I have so many "relatives" from different aspects of my life—college, travel, professional organizations, church—that the lines almost become blurred. In fact, when I introduce my friends to my actual relatives, my friends always ask, "Now, is this your *real* cousin?" I get strange looks from my relatives when that happens. They don't know about my proclivity to adopt new kinfolk.

Over the past year or so, I've been interacting quite a bit more than usual with some of my college buddies. Some of the occasions for our meetings have been happy and some have been sad, including the death of one friend. But even that sad occasion seemed to draw the rest of us closer together.

I guess the lesson I gained from all of this is to truly appreciate the people in your life. Whether they are blood relatives or love relatives, I am grateful for each and every one. Please take the time to let yours know that you appreciate them, as well.

FOLLOW THE MAP

*"I have an existential map. It has
'You are here' written all over it."*

STEVEN WRIGHT, COMEDIAN

When I was seven years old, my family drove from Chicago to Oakland to visit family and friends. It was a three-day odyssey each way. I still remember the view of the Great Salt Lake from the back of the car as we passed through Utah—I thought the white mountains were totally made of salt. Once we arrived, we were the special guests of the Queen of Fairyland, one of the first themed amusement parks in the United States, so I got to go to the front of every line in the park. (Friendship has its privileges!) I still have pictures of me in a white and powder blue dress with a powder blue balloon (what was my mother thinking?) in my hair.

During our drive to California and back, I was never concerned about whether we'd arrive safe and sound at our destination, because my father had a map he referred to often during the journey. We arrived safely and on time at our end point without incident.

But what if my dad had decided, instead, to forgo the map and just head west until we got to the Pacific Ocean? We might've eventually ended up in California, but would it have been San Francisco or San Diego? How long might it have taken? Would we have stopped and jumped out of the car every time we got distracted by something interesting on the side of the road? That would have slowed our progress immensely. We'd have been like the Steven Wright quote—all over the place.

Many times, we forgo using a map when we make plans for our future. Many of us put more work into planning a vacation than we do into planning our future. We head out with no clear sense of direction and are disappointed when we don't end up where we thought we'd be. We get distracted by all the things we see on the side of the road, and, frustrated, we often head back home.

MAP stands for make a plan. We all have goals that we want to achieve, but we also need a plan—a map—that will ensure we arrive at our goals in the most efficient manner. Businesses use a business plan to determine where they want their businesses to go and how they intend to get there. When you want to get your finances in order, you make a financial plan. Why not create a plan for your life to keep it on track? If you know where you're going, you're much more likely to get there.

Your life is a journey and your goals are your road map, helping to determine the best way to get there, the milestones, and the appropriate timing. If you are truly committed to your goals, do not shortchange yourself; put in the prework. Make a plan.

LESSON #68

There's an App for That

"It has become appallingly obvious that our technology has exceeded our humanity."

ALBERT EINSTEIN

Technology has invaded just about every part of our lives, and I love it, for the most part. I use my smartphone to wake up to the lovely sound of birds chirping. A knock lets me know that I have a text message. If I want to remember a meeting, I can be reminded by my phone, my laptop, or my tablet. I can take a picture with any number of devices; the one I'm least likely to use would be my actual camera. If I need to know how many calories are in my breakfast, guess what—there's an app for that, too! There seems to be an app, or computerized application, for whatever one might need to know or do. Without a smartphone, I don't know how I ever found my friends when we got separated in the mall.

It's truly an incredible thing, this instant availability of information. We can catch up on the latest news—political, Hollywood, or personal—from pretty much anywhere. It's really just a matter of choice: should I use my laptop, my smartphone, or my tablet?

But, at the risk of sounding like the ghost of Andy Rooney, has any of this technology made us any nicer? It seems to have made us more impatient and irritable. We read scathing posts on the Internet, where people anonymously snipe at each other in the comment sections. We *must* have all our information instantaneously, and we get annoyed if a website is running a bit slow. We are definitely worse at communicating with each other in a normal and civil manner and try to use as few words as possible when doing so. If we can manage to eke out a message using only random letters, so much the better. I once asked a high school student a question in a workshop and she answered, "IDK." Is it really that much trouble to say "I don't know"? It's the same number of syllables!

On top of butchering our spelling and speech, technology has had a profound impact on the modern dating scene. Most people are too lazy to pick up a phone—it's just easier to send an e-mail, text, tweet, or Facebook comment. But these messages can result in many arguments because of misinterpreted or misdelivered messages (trust me—I speak from experience). And how personal are these messages? I was reminded of a scene from the 2009 film *He's Just Not That Into You,* where one of the characters says: "I had this guy leave me a voice mail at work, so I called him at home and then he e-mailed me to my BlackBerry and so I texted to his cell. And then he e-mailed me to my home account . . . And now you just have to go around checking all these different portals just to get rejected by seven different technologies. It's exhausting." I know I'm tired just thinking about it.

We expect people to be on call 24-7, never giving others or ourselves a break from our smartphones or computers. Whatever happened to getting together with our actual friends face-to-face, instead of limiting our interactions to virtual ones on social media? Why are we ignoring the people right in front of us at the dinner table while checking texts and e-mail? I challenge you to start taking frequent technology breaks and experience what is going on in the real world.

Is there an app that makes people nicer to and more appreciative of each other? If there were one, would anybody use it? I don't know, but I am still a big fan of technology. It makes researching anything so much faster and more fun. I'll just try to stay away from the comments at the end of the blogs.

Now, go out, experience life, and make it a great day. And don't forget to be nice to people!

LESSON #69

GET OFF
YOUR DUFF

"Crap or get off the pot."

AMERICAN PROVERB

A funny thing happened at an event I hosted for women on finding one's life purpose. A woman named Katie, who was invited by a friend, shared a story with the group. She told us that although she hadn't known at the time what she'd be doing later that day (her friend hadn't invited her to the event yet), during her meditation that morning, she'd had a vision of her guardian angel, who came to visit her in the form of an African American woman (the attendee was Caucasian). The guardian angel told her to "Get off your *#%!" (A less polite word for "duff" was used.) At the event, we were talking about recognizing and living in your purpose and about following

275

through on your goals. I challenged the ladies to commit to action items and to create accountability for themselves. We all had a good laugh about Katie's story. I asked her if the guardian angel resembled anyone . . .

Although most of us have dreams of what we would like to have, do, or be in our lives, sometimes we just don't want to get moving—we don't want to get off our duffs. It isn't enough to just want something; we have to put in the necessary work to make it happen.

The hardest part of any endeavor is getting started. How many of us have had a great idea but just never got started? How many of us look back, with regret, at something we could have done but didn't? Mark Twain said, "Twenty years from now, you will be more disappointed by the things that you didn't do than by the ones you did do." It would be much better to try something and fail than to never even try, and spend the rest of your life focused on what-ifs.

Anyone who has ever ridden a bicycle knows that in order to move forward, you have to keep pedaling. Once you stop moving, you will fall off the bike. The same is true with our goals. Once we stop taking action, we will lose our forward momentum and our goals will fall off. We will become stagnant. Then discouragement will settle in. We might even begin to rationalize, "I knew it wouldn't work out. I don't know why I wasted time with that in the first place." It isn't that we can't achieve what we desire; it's just that we sometimes won't rise up and do what we need to do. The difference between successful people and everyone else is that successful people take action. And if they fail, guess what? They take a different action until they find the one that works.

Do you need to get off your "*#%" in any area of your life? In your health? Your finances? Your career or business? Your relationships? Are you settling for less than you want or deserve in any area of your life? If so, are you willing to take the steps necessary to make what you want a reality? Are you willing to get off your duff?

DREAM BIG DREAMS

"Some men see things as they are and say why?
I dream things that never were and say why not?"

EDWARD M. KENNEDY

I recently watched some of the activities surrounding the 50th anniversary of the March on Washington. What a testament to the power of a dream! Hearing speeches and seeing pictures from 1963 and from 2013 made me again realize what an impact each of us can make individually and how much more powerful we can be when we work together.

Whether it is personal or for the good of humanity, each of us has a dream—a vision of what we want for the future. Many people allow their dreams to remain dormant for their entire lives. The real power of having a dream is putting it into action. How many people would be happier and more fulfilled if they had the courage to truly live their dreams? Walt Disney, the ultimate dream creator, said, "All our dreams can come true, if we have the courage to pursue them."

Playing small is always the easiest course of action. I remember having been accused of doing just that in my corporate career. Someone told me that I was "playing small" so that I could make those around me feel comfortable. I remember being insulted at the time, but as time went on, I had to admit that I really didn't feel like I belonged there anymore. I realized I was holding myself back from my true potential, which pointed me in a totally different direction. I was getting more and more uncomfortable staying there and trying to blend in with everyone else, when I really wanted to follow my big dream. Without a big dream, we can never realize our potential. Edgar Allan Poe said, "Those who dream by day are cognizant of many things which escape those who dream only by night." I had a major daytime dream that I knew I wanted to achieve!

If you have a big dream, you will find that it will call to you louder and louder. If you ignore it, it might eventually quiet down, but you will be left feeling frustrated and unfulfilled, as if something is missing in your life. You might even see someone else living out your big dream and feel a twinge of envy that you didn't go that route yourself.

If you listen to the voice of your big dream, you can soon be on the road to self-actualization and fulfillment of your true life's purpose. If you listen to your big dream, it will take you places you never imagined. Don't worry if you've put your dream on the shelf. You can always dust it off again and get started. It is right there waiting for you.

Revisit your dreams on a daily basis. Share them with others so that you can create a network of support. Many of us keep our dreams to ourselves because we are afraid of what others might think and say. If you believe in your big dream, share it with others. The energy from your big dream will attract the support you need to keep it in motion.

The great thing about a big dream is that once it has been achieved, it will be replaced by another big dream. A true dreamer never stops exploring new horizons and creating new dreams. I'm already planning my next dream. How about you? It is the dreams that we have while we're awake that really count.

HOPE AND FAITH ARE TWINS

*"Hope is the ability to hear the music of the future.
Faith is the courage to dance to it today."*

PETER KUZMIC

I redecorated my bathroom recently, and one of my purchases was a beautiful plaque with the above quote on it. It was orange and brown—my favorite color combination—with a background that included a swirl of musical notes on a scale and two small butterflies. I bought it because the colors matched my bathroom, I loved what it said, and it was only $2. I can't pass up a bargain. Once I got the plaque home, I realized that it would fit perfectly in my "spa corner" (okay, so it's just a couple of rolled-up towels and some candles, but it feels spa-ish to me—you've got to do whatever works).

That plaque is a wonderful reminder each morning to appreciate every moment and to live today as if my life's dreams have already come true.

We all have things that we are hoping for in our future. We hear the music playing in the distance, but, for many of us, it remains just that—a distant hope. We never allow ourselves to actually dance to the music in our hearts because we do not have enough faith in what we are hoping for. We do not truly believe in the power of our dreams. If we exercise our faith muscles, we'll begin to realize that it is only by having the faith to step out into unknown waters and to pursue our dreams that we will actually bring what we want into fruition.

I read a book several years ago by John Ortberg called, *If You Want to Walk on Water, You've Got to Get Out of the Boat.* I loved the title and the premise of the book. We all have those safe harbors in our lives, but if we don't set sail, we'll never reach our desired destination. John A. Shedd said, "A ship in a harbor is safe—but that's not what ships are for."

Are you still hanging out in a safe harbor—out of fear, procrastination, or living in the past (fill in whatever floats your particular boat)? Are you suppressing your hopes when you should be harnessing your faith and stepping out into your future? Most people say they want to achieve certain things, but they will never put forth the effort to make those things happen. The only way your dreams will come true is if you decide to take action—when you decide to truly honor your commitment to have, be, and do all the things you've been hoping for. It's time for you to set sail!

GOALS BRIDGE THE GAP BETWEEN DREAMS AND REALITY

"If you don't know where you are going, you will probably end up somewhere else."

DR. LAURENCE J. PETER,
CREATOR OF THE PETER PRINCIPLE

There is a random but often quoted statistic that claims 3 percent of Americans have written goals. There is also a similar one that says 3 percent of Americans are wealthy. Now, I don't know where these numbers came from or if they are true. But I decided that just in case it is the same 3 percent, I'd better write my goals down. Why take chances? So, I started creating exhaustive lists, broken down into categories and subcategories. It all looked great. The problem with that was once I finished a list, I'd either save it and shut down my computer or print it out and stick it in a folder somewhere. How many of those goals do you really think got achieved? Not many.

We hear a lot of talk about how important it is to have goals. Goals do give you a road map to your future. They provide something to strive for—some point in the future to reach. But what exactly is a goal, and how do you know when you have achieved it?

According to the Oxford Dictionary, a goal is a "point marking end of race; object of effort or ambition; destination." In common terms, it's where you're trying to end up. If you are a sports fan, what would it be like to watch a football game where everybody was just running around the field? How confusing would that be? Okay, the whole game is confusing to me, but it helps to know that one team is trying to get to one end of the field and the other team is trying to get to the other end. In any game, there's always a goal line, a hoop, an end zone. There are no points for getting halfway. We can spend a whole lot of time running up and down the field of life not getting anywhere, if we don't have clear goals.

So, let's clarify . . .

"Get in shape" is not a goal. After all, round is a shape. Losing a certain amount of weight by a certain date through specific activities is a clear goal.

"Go back to school" is not a goal. Graduate with a certain degree by a certain date is a goal. A goal has to be clear in order to create the action steps needed to bring it into fruition.

"Save for retirement" is not a goal. Save a certain amount by a certain date with clear action steps is a goal.

Distinguish between your goals and your wishes or dreams. Your dreams are your vision of how you want to live, but only having clear goals will get you there. Don't be afraid of the space between your dreams and reality. Goal setting empowers you to bridge the gap between where you are and where you want to be. Putting your goals in writing shows your commitment to achieving the visions you have for your life. Clear goals will keep you moving forward despite the difficulty and obstacles. Even if you have failures along the way, you'll be moving in the right direction and will eventually arrive at your destination.

KEEP YOUR EYES ON THE PRIZE

"I have never felt that anything really mattered but the satisfaction of knowing that you stood for the things in which you believed and had done the very best you could."

ELEANOR ROOSEVELT

"Keep your eyes on the stars and your feet on the ground."

FRANKLIN DELANO ROOSEVELT

Talk about a power couple—Eleanor Roosevelt and FDR! They were life partners and distant cousins (who knew?). Both are often quoted because of their encouraging and empowering words. But they weren't just talk; history proves that their words were backed up by action. Both were people of great achievement. Her: first lady, activist, and diplomat; him: President, statesman, and military man. Both overcame immense personal challenges to become the historical figures we read about. She lost both parents by the age of ten and dealt with self-esteem issues because of her looks. He struggled with a paralytic illness as he ran for President of the United States. Neither let those challenges hold them back from achieving their goals. We should all have dreams that are larger than our obstacles!

What actions will you take now to bring your dreams into fruition? What new habits will you engage in to ensure your future success? A simple shift in thinking can make success a reality both personally and professionally. Maybe you want a bigger house, perhaps you want to launch a new business, or maybe you just want to fit into your favorite jeans. Whatever the goal, determine that today is the day you move one step closer to achieving it. Once you have clarity in your purpose, you will begin to move toward your ideal life, making choices that will jump-start your success.

I attended a networking event recently where attendees discussed their upcoming goals. It struck me when two of the organizers shared how they motivate themselves to exercise. One said that he lays his clothes out every night so that he'll have no excuse in the morning. The other indicated that he needed more motivation than that, so he actually sleeps in his workout clothes, including the shoes!

Their commitment definitely motivated me to jump up the next morning and hit the treadmill.

I am determined to live a life of purpose, passion, and faith and you should be, as well. Purpose never dies, so even if you are behind where you thought you'd be in your life's vision, it is never too late to begin. Laura Ingalls Wilder became a columnist at 44 years of age, and her Little House on the Prairie books were not published until she was in her 60s (whew—made it with time to spare!). Her purpose and passion were still alive.

Recently, 64-year-old Diana Nyad gained world attention and a world record on her fifth attempt to swim from Cuba to Florida. She swam from Havana to Key West for 53 hours without a shark cage. Upon her arrival, Nyad told reporters, "I got three messages. One is we should never, ever give up. Two is you never are too old to chase your dreams. Three is it looks like a solitary sport, but it's a team."

Tasks that seem difficult become easier when you keep your eyes on the prize—your ultimate goal. It takes faith that is bigger than your fears to push past the obstacles that hold you back from the success you seek. You might have had a slow start, but you can still have a great finish. Here's to a bright future! See you at the top.

OBEY THE CROSSING GUARD

"See, I am sending an angel ahead of you to guard you along the way and to bring you to the place I have prepared."

EXODUS 23:20

I spoke with a potential client recently who told me that she was feeling "stuck" when it came to her future life path. I think many of us have experienced that. Sometimes we're stuck because we truly don't know what we want to do. Other times, the "stuckness" comes through no lack of focus or effort on our part. We might just be required to wait for the right conditions and/or timing in order to receive optimal results. Like recently, when I got frustrated because a truck driver pulled into the fast lane ahead of me and drove right next to another truck for about a mile. It turned out that he was purposely making everyone slow down because he knew there was a speed trap ahead. Sometimes it seems that obstacles come up that slow our progress toward what we want.

Have you ever felt that you were being made to wait for something you really wanted in life—a new job, a major client, that big house you always dreamed of, a spouse? We've all felt that way at one time or another. Waiting is frustrating. We know where we're trying to go, but it often seems that something is blocking our way to getting there. It isn't that we aren't working hard; it just isn't happening for us in the way we'd like it to.

Life is full of traffic. Think back to when you were in grade school and had to cross the street. Sometimes the crossing guard would hold up that big red stop sign and blow a loud whistle to halt the traffic so that you could cross the street right away. At other times, she would stop you from moving forward and you couldn't figure out why. A few seconds later, a car or truck would pass. Then, with a gap in traffic, she would lead you across the street. From the crossing guard's higher elevation (what were you, four feet tall in second grade?), she could see what you couldn't at the time and knew when it was safe to proceed. Even now, as adult drivers, we are still subject to the direction of the crossing guards who serve as traffic management officers.

I believe that we each have a celestial "Crossing Guard." Throughout our lives, this Crossing Guard looks out for us in a number of situations:

- **We have a blind spot.** There could be traffic approaching that we can't see. Sometimes there is something down the road that might be harmful to us. We can't see it yet, but the Crossing Guard can, from a higher vantage point. Although we get frustrated at having to slow down or even stop, it is better for us in the long run.

- **There is a lot of traffic.** Most of us are multitaskers. We often have so much going on that we are not doing anything optimally. We juggle so much at once that we put ourselves at risk of burning out. That is when the Crossing Guard tells us to slow down—to relax and focus on one thing at a time.

- **There is a necessary detour in the road.** We might have to take a circuitous route to avoid a pitfall or, perhaps, go out of our way to help someone else who is in need. The Crossing Guard directs us through necessary detours in our route, at times putting out signs and markers to steer us in the right direction. Having control over situations that we can't control, if necessary, the Crossing Guard will activate warning signals and even manually lift or lower a crossing gate to allow us to pass. (Ever had a major obstacle just disappear?)

- **Construction is needed.** Sometimes we think we are ready for the things we want to happen in our lives, but if we were to get what we wanted right then, we might not be prepared to handle it. We might need to be resurfaced or have our potholes filled before moving down our road of purpose.

- **The weather is hazardous**. Life can get pretty slippery. Issues arise with family, work, health, and so on, and sometimes we just have to stop and address those issues. When the weather is at its worst, the Crossing Guard's job is even more important, as it is harder for us to see things clearly enough to make good decisions alone.

- **There is an emergency situation.** The Crossing Guard stands in harm's way, warning us of approaching hazards, to ensure that we don't sustain any injuries. Signage, hand signals, and flares let us know to avoid an area where danger exists.

- **We might be breaking the rules of the road.** Sometimes we get out of line—moving too fast, going when it isn't our turn, or traveling outside our lane—and the Crossing Guard has to put us in check. We might get stopped or even get punished with a ticket if we get out of line, so that we learn a lesson about putting ourselves and others in danger.

Are you truly "stuck" or just waiting on your path to purpose? Happily, sometimes the Crossing Guard halts the things in our lives that block our paths to purpose, so that we can keep moving smoothly along. But, at other times, we are made to stop and wait for a better time to move in the direction we want to go. Next time you get frustrated because things don't seem to be happening quite quickly enough, remember that it might just be that the Crossing Guard is clearing a path for you. So stop, look, and listen.

JUST DON'T LOOK DOWN

*"Never look down to test the ground before taking
your next step; only he who keeps his eye fixed
on the far horizon will find the right road."*

DAG HAMMARSKJÖLD

Last fall, I went on another one of my "all-girls" trips (12 of us) to Hilton Head Island. One of the fun things we did was rent bicycles for the week. Most mornings, we went riding through the neighborhoods and on the beach. Some of the paths to the beach were very narrow, and we found that we tended to get wobbly when we rode on those routes, especially when the trails sloped upward or downward or had sharp turns. It was a bit scary at times. Fortunately, one of the ladies noticed that if she kept her eyes focused in front of her on where she was going, rather than looking down at the ground, her bike remained steady. In addition, the scenery was much better looking toward the beach and the ocean than it was looking at the dirt. Overall, it made the ride much more enjoyable.

Sometimes in life, we find ourselves on paths that seem very narrow and difficult to navigate. Life can definitely take us on some ups and downs with a few sharp turns thrown in for good measure. When we focus on those hills and valleys, it is easy to let fear and temporary distractions make us wobbly in our purpose. Instead, we should look forward to all the wonderful things that are in our destiny. Here are a few things to remember so that you keep yourself steady:

- **Don't look at the ground!** Your current life situation might seem overwhelming. If you are going through struggles in your career, finances, relationships, or health, it is easy to allow fear and uncertainty to absorb all your thoughts and dictate your actions and reactions. You might doubt that your path is secure and start to wobble a bit. When sitting in a chair that you've never seen, you don't test it out before you sit; you just plop down in faith that the chair will hold you.

We have to have similar faith in a future that we cannot see or test in advance. Step out in faith, knowing that the ground you're on is steady and that your path has already been laid out.

- **Focus on a point ahead.** Staying focused on your goals instead of on your current life situation will help you to steady yourself. What positive things are in your future that you need to stay focused on? Is there a significant goal or life event that you are working toward? If you don't already have your goals for the next year set, this is a great time to create them. Focus on what is to come instead of what you're going through.

- **Take joy in the horizon.** Has your attention ever been captured by a beautiful sunset or by the line that divides the water from the sky? It is the things that we look toward that engage us, enrapture us, and lift our spirits. Look toward the beautiful horizon that is your future. If you can't imagine it in your mind, make a vision board that you can actually look at, to encourage yourself.

Use that mental or physical picture of your future to cheer you when you are feeling wobbly. Trust me, it will make the ride much more fun!

It isn't where you are now, but where you're going that is really important. Stay focused on the future and create your goals based on where you're trying to end up, not based on where you are now. As Sean Covey said, we have to "begin with the end in mind." When determining where we want to go in life, it's important to have clear, measurable goals. Setting *smarter* goals will keep you moving in a positive direction.

Here's to smooth paths!

CLOSING THOUGHTS— LILLIAN'S STORY

Last week, I was flying from North Platte, Nebraska, back home to Chicago. I arrived at the airport very early (shocking, I know!) and had some time to kill before they would announce our gate. I spotted a family in the small waiting area: a petite older lady, no more than 5'1", with whom I discovered were her son and daughter-in-law. I couldn't help laughing, because the entire time she and her son teased and joked with each other. It was easy to see how much love was between them. Stating that she was 90 years young, the lady happily sprinted across the floor in the tiny terminal, arms bent at her sides, to demonstrate that she was still in good shape despite her years. She kept up her cheerful banter the whole while, causing her son to comment to his wife jokingly, "I feel sorry for whoever sits

299

next to her on the plane. They will have to listen to her talk the whole time." I thought she was adorable.

As we went through security, she was the only one of the six or so passengers flying with us who was selected by the TSA for a body search. During the pat down, she joked, "I'm enjoying this! I haven't been rubbed on in a long time." She came over and sat down next to me and joked with everyone at the gate. She explained her outgoing personality: "Shoot, I have to act tough to make up for my height!"

I don't usually talk to strangers on planes, but she had such a beautiful spirit and sense of playfulness. And ever since my mom passed away, I've found myself drawn to the company of older ladies. The plane was not full, so I purposely sat across the aisle from her. I noticed that, when she sat down, she formed her arms in a circle and rocked them back and forth, like she was rocking a baby, then dropped them to her lap. Interesting. We were about to take off and I noticed that her seat belt was not fastened, so I helped her fasten it and we began to talk.

"I'm afraid of heights, but not on a plane," she said. I admitted that the same is true for me. "Whenever I get on a plane," she said, "I'm never afraid. I just sit down and do my arms like this." She demonstrated the baby-rocking motion that I'd noticed earlier. "That reminds me that I'm safe in God's arms. So, I don't have anything to be afraid of."

After a bit of conversation, I asked this feisty, fun little lady her name. "Lillian Welden," she said. And to clarify the spelling, she explained, "not Weldon. I'm not done welding." I laughed. "My grandmother's name was Lillian," I told her. "Your grandmother must've been old, to have a name like that," she remarked. She spoke with animated facial expressions and had a sense of childlike wonder and excitement—she was amazed by the clouds that looked like snow, the sky that looked like a lake, and even how the plane managed to stay in the air.

Every so often, Lillian would tap my arm and start talking again. Usually I read or play games on a flight, but I didn't pull out my book or Kindle, even after she went to sleep, because I didn't want to discourage her from conversation. I just looked out the window and admired the clouds, seeing them through her eyes as well as mine.

I found out that Lillian's husband died 13 years ago and that her son insisted that she call him every day by a certain time to check in, so that he'd know she was all right. If she didn't call on time, she'd receive a call from him. "I'm just checking in," Lillian said gruffly, laughingly imitating her son's voice. She also told me about her other children (she had five total), of whom she was very proud.

Entranced by her and wanting to know as much as possible, I asked her where she was from and where she lived now. Lillian was from a small town in Mississippi—Bovina, I think she said—but now lives in Nebraska. "I've found that there's something good in every place. And there's something bad in every place. There are good people in every race and there are bad people in every race. My daddy always said that we are all the same. And I believe that."

Before I knew it, we landed in Denver. I had to rush to catch my connecting flight home, but before I did, Lillian leaned over and said, "It was so nice meeting you and talking to you. You're a real nice lady for a young'un." She continued, "When all your children get the senior citizen's discount, you know you're old."

"I enjoyed meeting you, too." I laughed. "And you're not old. You are *full of life.*"

"I love life," she replied. "Every minute of it."

I reflected on my conversation with Lillian as I sat in the brand-new, totally full, 240-seat jumbo jet with special lighting (are the seats getting smaller or are my hips getting wider?), headed to Chicago's O'Hare Airport. Ninety years old, so full of life and still marveling at the world. I think I want to be like Lillian when I grow up—*if* I grow up. By the way, that tiny, 19-seater plane ride was one of the smoothest I've ever experienced.

I guess the bonus lesson I'd like to leave with you is to appreciate every moment that life offers you, just like Lillian does. Embrace life with childlike exuberance, always looking at the positives. And, if you can help it, never grow up. I sure don't intend to.

Thanks for supporting the book.
Wishing you much future success!
Feel free to sign up for the "EmPOWERed to . . ."
newsletter at www.talayahstovall.com and
follow me on Twitter @talayahstovall.

ABOUT THE AUTHOR

Talayah G. Stovall, president of TGrace and managing director of Vision Catalyst Consulting, is an author, speaker, trainer, and certified life purpose coach. Her mission is to empower people to use their passion to live in their purpose. Talayah inspires people to utilize their God-given abilities to achieve their personal and professional goals and increase their life satisfaction. She specializes in coaching individuals and groups to set and achieve their life goals through various programs, including her signature *5 Weeks to Personal Breakthrough,* customized personal and professional development workshops, and her "EmPOWERed to . . ." newsletter and radio show.

Talayah brings a wealth of training and life experience into her work. She has experienced career and life transitions herself and has learned the power of reinvention. With an undergraduate degree in business administration and a master of business administration in marketing, she spent over 16 years in the banking industry before leaving to follow her true passion. In addition to being an entrepreneur, she is currently an adjunct instructor at Columbia College in Chicago, where she teaches public speaking.

Talayah's lifelong passion for writing and speaking led her to complete her first book, *Crossing the Threshold: Opening Your Door to Successful Relationships.* She also has an e-book: *150 Important Questions You Should Ask Before You Say "I Do."* Talayah also has two motivational audio CDs: *P.U.M.P. It Up! (Pursue Your Passion, Utilize Your Uniqueness, Make a Plan, and Persevere with Positivity)* and *7 Secrets to Ignite Your Dreams* (with business partner, Kiela Smith-Upton).

Talayah is a member of Toastmasters International and a lifetime member of the National Black MBA Association. She is on the board of the Chicago Youth Centers–Rebecca Crown Center and a member of the trustee board of the Vernon Park Church of God. She serves as a volunteer mentor with the Chicagoland Entrepreneurial Center's Future Founders program. She also served as the Chicago regional director of the Greatness Center, with motivational speaker Les Brown, and as the Chicago local director of FraserNet PowerNetworking.

Talayah was recognized in the 2013 article, "Who's Who in Academia," in the 2007–2008 Emerald Who's Who among Executives and Professionals, has twice appeared in *Ebony* magazine, and has twice been recognized in Outstanding Young Women of America. She is a native and current resident of Chicago, Illinois.

To book Talayah for a speaking engagement or workshop facilitation, to find out about upcoming events, or to sign up for the "EmPOWERed to . . ." newsletter, visit www.talayahstovall.com.

Share your feedback on the book or your own personal light bulb moments on Twitter @talayahstovall (use the hashtag #LightBulbMoments).

◀▼▶

Hay House Titles of Related Interest

YOU CAN HEAL YOUR LIFE, the movie,
starring Louise Hay & Friends
(available as a 1-DVD program and an expanded 2-DVD set)
Watch the trailer at: www.LouiseHayMovie.com

THE SHIFT, the movie,
starring Dr. Wayne W. Dyer
(available as a 1-DVD program and an expanded 2-DVD set)
Watch the trailer at: www.DyerMovie.com

◂▾▸

A DAILY DOSE OF SANITY: A Five-Minute Soul Recharge for Every Day of the Year, by Alan Cohen

EXCUSES BEGONE!: How to Change Lifelong, Self-Defeating Thinking Habits, by Dr. Wayne W. Dyer

NOTHING CHANGES UNTIL YOU DO: A Guide to Self-Compassion and Getting Out of Your Own Way, by Mike Robbins

SHIFT HAPPENS: How to Live an Inspired Life . . . Starting Right Now!, by Robert Holden, Ph.D.

All of the above are available at your local bookstore,
or may be ordered by contacting Hay House (see next page).

We hope you enjoyed this Hay House book. If you'd like to receive our online catalog featuring additional information on Hay House books and products, or if you'd like to find out more about the Hay Foundation, please contact:

Hay House, Inc., P.O. Box 5100, Carlsbad, CA 92018-5100
(760) 431-7695 or (800) 654-5126
(760) 431-6948 (fax) or (800) 650-5115 (fax)
www.hayhouse.com® • www.hayfoundation.org

Published and distributed in Australia by: Hay House Australia Pty. Ltd.,
18/36 Ralph St., Alexandria NSW 2015 • *Phone:* 612-9669-4299
Fax: 612-9669-4144 • www.hayhouse.com.au

Published and distributed in the United Kingdom by:
Hay House UK, Ltd., Astley House, 33 Notting Hill Gate, London
W11 3JQ • *Phone:* 44-20-3675-2450 • *Fax:* 44-20-3675-2451
www.hayhouse.co.uk

Published and distributed in the Republic of South Africa by:
Hay House SA (Pty), Ltd., P.O. Box 990, Witkoppen 2068
Phone/Fax: 27-11-467-8904 • www.hayhouse.co.za

Published in India by: Hay House Publishers India, Muskaan Complex,
Plot No. 3, B-2, Vasant Kunj, New Delhi 110 070 • *Phone:* 91-11-4176-1620
Fax: 91-11-4176-1630 • www.hayhouse.co.in

Distributed in Canada by: Raincoast Books, 2440 Viking Way,
Richmond, B.C. V6V 1N2 • *Phone:* 1-800-663-5714
Fax: 1-800-565-3770 • www.raincoast.com

◄▼►

Take Your Soul on a Vacation

Visit www.HealYourLife.com® to regroup, recharge, and reconnect with your own magnificence.Featuring blogs, mind-body-spirit news, and life-changing wisdom from Louise Hay and friends.

Visit www.HealYourLife.com today!

Free e-newsletters from Hay House, the Ultimate Resource for Inspiration

Be the first to know about Hay House's dollar deals, free downloads, special offers, affirmation cards, giveaways, contests, and more!

 Get exclusive excerpts from our latest releases and videos from **Hay House Present Moments**.

 Enjoy uplifting personal stories, how-to articles, and healing advice, along with videos and empowering quotes, within **Heal Your Life**.

 Have an inspirational story to tell and a passion for writing? Sharpen your writing skills with insider tips from **Your Writing Life**.

Sign Up Now!

Get inspired, educate yourself, get a complimentary gift, and share the wisdom!

http://www.hayhouse.com/newsletters.php

Visit www.hayhouse.com to sign up today!

   HealYourLife.com